GUIDE TO A
STRESS FREE
MOVE

Century 21® Editors
and Judy Ramsey

**Real Estate
Education Company®**
a division of Dearborn Financial Publishing, Inc.

This publication is designed to provide accurate and authoritative information in regard to the subject matter covered. It is sold with the understanding that the publisher is not engaged in rendering legal, accounting, or other professional service. If legal advice or other expert assistance is required, the services of a competent professional person should be sought.

Executive Editor: Cynthia A. Zigmund
Managing Editor: Jack Kiburz
Interior Design: Lucy Jenkins
Cover Designer: ST & Associates
Typesetting: Elizabeth Pitts

©1997 by Dearborn Financial Publishing, Inc.®

Published by Real Estate Education Company®,
a division of Dearborn Financial Publishing, Inc.®

Printed in the United States of America

97 98 99 10 9 8 7 6 5 4 3 2 1

Library of Congress Cataloging-in-Publication Data

Century 21 guide to a stress-free move / Century 21 editors and Judy
    Ramsey.
        p.   cm.
    Includes index.
    ISBN 0-7931-2397-6 (pbk.)
    1. Moving, Household—Handbooks, manuals, etc. I. Ramsey, Judy.
II. Century 21 (Firm)
TX307.C45   1997
648'.9—dc21   96-52846
                                                               CIP

Find This Book Useful for Your Real Estate Needs?

Discover all the bestselling CENTURY 21® Guides:

CENTURY 21® Guide to Buying Your Home

CENTURY 21® Guide to Choosing Your Mortgage

CENTURY 21® Guide to Inspecting Your Home

CENTURY 21® Guide to Selling Your Home

CENTURY 21® Guide to Buying Your First Home

CENTURY 21® Guide to Remodeling Your Home

CONTENTS

PREFACE

Americans are on the move. This year, you're one of the millions who are moving. You're transferring, relocating, retiring, or starting over across town or across the world.

You've got a lot of work ahead of you. But there are many ways to make the tasks associated with moving easier.

That's where this *CENTURY 21® Guide to a Stress-Free Move* can help. It contains help for the experienced mover as well as the novice.

This book includes an overview of the moving process; how to estimate the cost of your move; how to learn more about your new neighborhood, city, or state; and how to organize a stress-free move. It leads you through the steps of deciding how much of the moving job to tackle yourself and how much to leave to the professionals. It discusses working with a moving company as well as how to move on a budget. It is full of packing and loading tips and includes a whole chapter on the emotional aspects of moving.

The 43 Money-$aving Tips will help keep your move from squeezing your budget too tightly. Each chapter ends with answers to commonly asked questions on how to make moving day fun—or at least less painful.

All of us in the CENTURY 21® System—*the* source for homeowner information and services—wish you the very best in your journey from your old home to your new home. We also wish you happiness in your new home.

Acknowledgments

Judy Ramsey gratefully acknowledges the help of Atlas Van Lines, U-Haul, Paul Arpin Van Lines, American Red Ball, Wheaton World Wide Moving, Interstate Van Lines, Ryder, Stevens Worldwide Van Lines, Allied Van Lines, and the American Movers Conference in researching this book.

CHAPTER 1

Understanding the Moving Process

Americans are on the move. Of the 255 million people in the United States, as many as 50 million of them move into new homes each year. A large majority of those moves occur within the same county. The rest are across the state, across the country, or even halfway around the world. The average American can expect to move more than ten times during a lifetime. For every couple who lives in just one or two homes throughout their marriage, another couple calls a new house or apartment, and maybe even a new town, home every two or three years.

No matter how many times a family relocates, each new move presents new challenges. Is this the time to dispose of Grandma's collection of salt and pepper shakers from around the world? Will the antique wicker chair survive one more trip? Is it time to throw away the iron that only works on one setting and buy a new one at the other end? Is there a good doctor or dentist in the new town? Will Mark qualify for the football team at his new school? Does the new school offer a good music program for Jan? Will your new neighbors be as friendly as the Fosters and the Mitchells?

When you are facing a move, the questions and complications seem endless. Will you do it all yourself or will you hire a moving company to plan, pack, and transport all your goods? Or a bit of both options? With some organization and planning, the moving process will become less formidable.

The Steps to Moving

Step 1—Deciding to move. The first big decision is whether to move or not. Perhaps you have outgrown your current home. A cozy one-bedroom apartment may fill the needs of a young couple, but the addition of a child or two quickly turns cozy into overcrowded. At the other end of the spectrum, if you have already raised your family and no longer wish to shovel snow every winter, it may be time to search out the ideal retirement community and home. Or your boss just offered you the chance to take over the Phoenix branch of the business, with a substantial raise when you increase profits by 20 percent. Other valid reasons for moving include changing climate for health reasons, meeting family needs, improving your living conditions, divorce, death, and searching for a better life.

Step 2—Telling the family. Moving is commonly recognized as a high-stress experience. Moving from one home to another within a neighborhood causes stress. Moves from one community to another dramatically increase the stress because they involve many more changes. In addition to changing homes, such moves usually mean changing jobs, schools, churches, friends, and other factors that are also acknowledged stress inducers. You can help minimize the stress to your family by keeping them informed of your moving plans.

Tell the family of the move as soon as possible. Depending upon the ages of your children, involve them in the initial decision to move. Even younger children should be told as soon as possible so that they have time to adjust to the idea of leaving a familiar home, neighborhood, and friends for an unknown future. A family meeting offers a positive time for sharing moving details. Don't overload young children with unnecessary details, but all children need to know the reasons for the move. Even a three-year-old can grasp the idea that Mommy or Daddy has to go to a new place to work. Be prepared to tell the children something about what they can expect at the new location. If it is a new neighborhood in the same city, will there be a playground or park nearby? Will they walk to the new school? If it is a new part of the country, will they get to play in snow for the first time? Children will be apprehensive about any move and you must respect and alleviate their fears as much as possible.

Step 3—Finding a new home. Once the whole family knows of the need to move, you can begin the search for a new house. Whether you need to move within your current neighborhood or across the country, a good real estate agent can help simplify the process.

☞ **Money-$aving Tip #1** *If you have a home to sell, you want to get the best price possible. To do that, your home needs to be in top shape. You will want to perform or contract for repairs, refresh old paint, spruce up landscaping, replace that leaky roof or gutters, and generally make your home present its best face.*

Your real estate agent can make suggestions on what needs to be done to command the best selling price and to make your home show to its best advantage. Your agent will also help you set a fair price for your home. All family members can help, especially with keeping the house clean and uncluttered for showing to prospective buyers.

With your home cleaned, repaired, and ready for sale, you can concentrate on finding the perfect new home.

☞ **Money-$aving Tip #2** *A good real estate agent with connections all across the country can help you find a new home in your price range to love in your old neighborhood or on the opposite coast.*

You can help your agent by making a list of all the things you require in your new home. Do you need three bedrooms or four? Do you want an eat-in kitchen and a separate dining room? Do you need garden space or room for a horse? Do you want to walk to the shopping mall or stroll country lanes? Do any family members have conditions that require wheelchair access or other special arrangements? What is your housing budget? A good real estate agent will want to know all this and more so that the housing search will be as efficient and as quick as possible.

Step 4—Planning the move. Even before finding your dream house you can begin to plan your move. The more time you have before your move, the easier you can make it. But even with short notice, a well-planned move can go smoothly and with a minimum of stress and disruption to family life. Your plans will adjust as necessary to your time frame.

If you have a choice, schedule your move for off-peak times. Moving companies and truck rental companies are far busier during the summer—approximately 45 percent of all moves take place in June, July, and August. Roads will also be busiest then with vacationers and sightseers. While it will be easier to schedule a winter move, you must also consider weather conditions and routes that may lead you through snow country. Avoid moving on a weekend if possible. Not only will scheduling be easier, but banks, utilities, and other services will be open and available to serve your needs.

If you have plenty of time before your move, begin to de-clutter your home as soon as you even think about moving. The longer you have lived in your current home, the more important this step. A few years ago the Martin family decided that within the next year they would return to the Southwest after several years of living in Pennsylvania in a large home with a full basement and a two-car garage. With several years' worth of, "If you don't need it, put it in the basement; somebody might want it someday," the Martins knew they had accumulated far too much to move. In the fall, Mrs. Martin purchased a new 32-gallon trash can and the family vowed to fill it once a week with things to get rid of. Some objects were identified for a spring yard sale, some were bound for the dump, and others were labeled for give-away to a charity's thrift store. By spring, several loads had been donated to charity, several pickup loads had been taken to the dump, and enough for a profitable moving sale remained. What was left from the garage sale was donated to the thrift store and the Martins were left with only the items they felt were really worth moving.

Your moving budget will likely dictate how much of the move you will tackle yourself, unless your employer or new employer is footing the bill for relocation. The majority of moves are do-it-yourself projects, involving doing all your own packing and loading, using your own, borrowed, or rented vehicles. You may decide to do all your own packing and have a moving company load, transport, and unload your possessions. Or you may have a moving company do it all from start to finish at your own or your employer's expense. If you are unsure, get price quotes from both rental truck or trailer suppliers and moving companies. Get several estimates to compare for the best price and service.

☞ **Money-$aving Tip #3** *Even if you have a moving company move all your possessions, you can save money by doing part of the job, such as all the packing yourself.*

Many other things you can do to prepare for a smooth move are outlined and listed in Chapter 7, including creating a moving calendar that will remind you to transfer school and medical records, turn off utilities at the old house and on at the new house. Noting future tasks on a calendar frees your mind to focus on current tasks.

Step 5—Executing the move. Make moving an adventure, whether it is a one-day task or a five-day drive to your new hometown. With careful planning and organization, you will know what to expect come moving day. If you're just moving across town, it may be easiest to have a friend or relative watch small children and pets for the day. Then when the heavy moving is finished, make a big production of the children's arrival at the new house. Let even the youngest help settle into his or her new room and explore the new house and yard. Take a walk through the neighborhood and introduce yourselves to anyone you meet. The small amount of time this will take will help your children to begin feeling at home and will give you a brief break from unloading boxes and barrels.

If your drive is more than a couple hours, break it into manageable segments, remembering that adults, as well as children, travel more comfortably with frequent stops for stretching and exercising. When you reach your new city, take the time to do at least a short sightseeing expedition before tackling the move into the house. Again, as with a move within a city, give the kids time to explore the house, yard, and neighborhood.

Step 6—After the move. Once you have begun to settle the household following your move, you can make the transition to your new neighborhood or city less traumatic by quickly getting to know the area and getting your personal and family business started with new schools, banks, doctors, organizations, and churches. Get your driver's license and license plates for your new state. Register to vote. Go to PTA meetings. Take the kids to visit the museum or the zoo. Help them search out sources of previous interest and also help them learn about new interests. The more quickly you become involved in your new community, the sooner you will call it home.

An International Move

An international move requires special consideration and special determination on the part of the people lucky enough to try such an adventure. Each step of the moving process will be more complex and many may include language barriers. More paperwork will be involved because most international moves require a passport and supporting documents. Schools will be harder to find. Extra regulations govern moving animals into foreign countries. Cultural differences may cause questions or difficulties. Even your appliances will require special adapters in most other countries! Finding new doctors, dentists, and other medical specialists will be complicated. But it can all be done and could be the beginning of the adventure of a lifetime.

How *Your Agent Can Help*

A well-qualified real estate agent can help you determine a fair price for your home. The agent will gather information on comparable homes in your area and help you set a price that will be attractive to buyers and still bring you the best price on your investment. Your agent can also suggest repairs or improvements that will add buyer appeal and value. A good agent will list your home with the local multiple listing service, advertise it in local publications, show it to qualified buyers, and encourage other agents to show it to qualified buyers.

At the same time, an agent with national connections can help you in your search for a home in your new location. Agents with offices throughout the country can contact their associates and offer you descriptions, photos, and even videos of homes available where you are moving. With computer networks, fax machines, and telephones, the home search can be completed nearly as efficiently as if you were looking right next door. Your agent will be able to help you get an idea of the cost of housing in your new city, as well as supply general information on the area and its cost of living.

Commonly Asked Questions

Q. Children adapt quickly. Should we wait until all our plans are settled to tell the children about our move?

A. No. It's not easy for children to adjust to a move. Their whole world is changing and they feel insecure. If a move is sprung on them quickly, they will be even more bewildered. Tell children well ahead of the move and include them in plans and preparation. Be sure to talk about the positive aspects of the move, but also to acknowledge their fears and negative feelings.

Q. I've moved before. Why worry about my move weeks ahead of time?

A. Planning can take much of the stress out of moving. It can also reduce the workload and expense. It may be easier and less expensive to replace some furniture, appliances, and even smaller items rather than to pack and move them.

CHAPTER 2

Discovering Your Destination

When you're considering moving to another area, or when you have to move whether you want to or not, you want to know about the place where you are going. You can learn a lot about a new town, state, or country even if you can't visit personally.

You and your family will want to know how big the town is, what the schools offer, how hot it gets in the summer, and how cold it gets in the winter. You'll want to know what job opportunities exist and what colleges and universities are nearby. You'll want to know what the people there do for fun. Is it a sports-minded community? How is the fishing? Is there a cultural center? Museum?

In one of your family meetings, you might ask everyone what they want to know about their prospective hometown. Then you can appoint or ask for a volunteer to gather information for everyone.

This chapter offers a few tips for discovering what your new neighborhood, city, county, state, or even country will be like. Whatever the distance you move, there is something to learn about the area.

Learning about Your New Neighborhood

If you are moving from one neighborhood to another in the same town, or even in a nearby or adjoining town, you probably already know a great deal about your new area. But you may want to know more specifically what to expect in the new neighborhood.

Because you are near your new home, you can easily learn more about it. Spend some time there driving around to get a basic introduction. Then get out of the car and walk, especially the few blocks surrounding your new home. Introduce yourself to the neighbors. Ask them questions. Find out who else lives nearby. Do they hold an annual neighborhood picnic or yard sale? Where do the kids play? Do most of the parents work away from home, leaving the neighborhood quiet during the day? Where is the nearest or best pharmacy, supermarket, and take-out pizza parlor or Chinese restaurant? Is there a Neighborhood Watch program?

Next, talk with officials. Call city hall and find out who represents your neighborhood at the city council. Call your city council representative and ask about issues that concern your neighborhood. Is there a plan to improve sidewalks soon (at homeowner expense)? Is anyone trying to rezone and change the atmosphere and structure of the area?

Talk to the police department or watch the local newspaper to learn about crime in the neighborhood. If there is a problem, what is being done about it? How can you help?

The local newspaper will also help you learn what is happening in the neighborhood. Watch for club news and other areas that might interest you once you move.

Visit your city's tourist information center and pick up brochures about the neighborhood and the town. You may learn a number of things about the town you have lived in for several years!

Learning about Your New City

Moving to a new city can be exciting; you can make it an adventure. Think about all the new things you can see and do. And by learning about the city or town beforehand, you can be ready to settle in quickly and become involved in your new hometown.

Even if you can't visit before your move, you can learn about your new city through maps, booklets, books, tourist brochures, and more. To start, go to your local bookstore or library and check out the travel section. You might find a book about your new city or at least a section about it in a more general book. Look for maps, too. Try a map store if you live in or near a large city. Topographical maps of the area will help you visualize the terrain in and around your new city.

Call or write to the chamber of commerce in your destination city. They should be happy to send you a package of information about the city and surrounding area. Their package will probably include a city map; information about the climate; living conditions; some economic statistics; information about schools, churches, local businesses, and organizations; and information about utilities and other helpful topics. You can simply ask for whatever information they have, or you can request specific information that will be helpful to members of your family.

If you are moving for a new or relocated job, ask your employer for help. Many large employers offer help relocating employees. They may have information about lots of things you have questions about.

Order a phone book for your new city or ask someone for a recently outdated one. Or check your local library; some have phone books for other areas. Phone books contain all kinds of useful information. You can scan the yellow pages to get an idea of the types of businesses in the town. You can make specific contacts to request more data. You can call the schools that your children will attend and talk with a counselor or the principal. You can do a preliminary survey of the medical and other professionals and start establishing your new circle of reference. You can call the utility companies to hook up your electricity and phone service the day before you arrive in town!

Order a mail subscription to the local newspaper. Read about your new town, the politics, the events, the sports, the schools, and society. Learn about the people by reading the letters to the editor. Scan the display advertising to learn about local shopping. Read the classified ads for jobs, a car to replace the one you are leaving behind, and lots of other information.

Make the new city your own. Start to know it now.

☞ **Money-$aving Tip #4** *Even if you can't afford to visit before your move, you can learn about your new city through maps, booklets, books, tourist brochures, and more. Instead of a trip, subscribe to the newspaper in the new city.*

Learning about Your New County

Learning about your new county is much the same as learning about your new city. Your local bookstore or library may carry books that include both history and current affairs about your new county. Or try calling a bookstore or two within your new county. They are likely to have regional books you cannot obtain elsewhere, such as a county history or diaries of local people.

The county courthouse will have records about all kinds of transactions within the county, including land and home sales. There you can find the history of your new home and the history of other homes around yours. For a small fee, you can probably get a copy of a map of your new home or neighborhood. Other county maps may be available also.

Learning about Your New State

As your search for knowledge becomes broader, more resources will be available. Again, start with your bookstore or library. If there is nothing on the shelves, ask about other resources. Obviously, there are books available on all 50 states, but you may have to ask your bookstore or library to order the one you want.

A map store should have available maps of all states.

The state's department of tourism should be another good source of information. Call or write them and ask for maps and information about the state in general and specifically for information about the region of the state you will be moving to. Learning about things in other parts of the state will help you create a list of fun things to do on weekends after you get settled in your new home.

If you are not moving to one of the largest cities in the state, subscribe anyway to a daily newspaper from a nearby large city. It will include regional and state news as well as local, national, and international.

Learning about Your New Country

When you plan to make your new home in a foreign country, you will want to know as much as you can about the country, the people, the customs, and many other topics before you move.

Once again, books offer many answers. Head for the travel section at your bookstore or library. Look for current titles because laws concerning work permits, visas, and other topics can change quickly and you need up-to-date information.

You can find books that discuss the legal aspects of working and living in another country, as well as social customs, educational opportunities, shopping, language, and much more. The more informed you are about the country you are moving to, the more quickly you will feel at home and part of the community. And learning about the culture of another country is fascinating!

The U.S. State Department can furnish you with information you need about passports, visas, export permits, and more. You can also contact the U.S. embassy in your destination country.

Using Your Computer to Learn about Your Destination

You can learn a great deal about your destination if your computer has online capabilities. You can get acquainted with the climate and topography, employment opportunities, shopping, and many other things. You might even chat with someone in your destination city.

Chapter 11 gives more information about using your computer to prepare for your move.

How Your Agent Can Help

Your local real estate agent can put you in touch with an agent in your destination city who can gather much of the previously mentioned information for you, in addition to helping you purchase a home in the new city.

If your agent is connected to the Internet and able to supply you with the computer research into your new town, either make a list of specific questions you would like answered about the new town or try to be on hand when the search is completed.

How Your Mover Can Help

If you hire a moving company to transport your belongings to a new city, ask about any relocation services offered. Some large moving companies will furnish you with factual information about the geography, climate, government, housing, utilities, education, banks, churches, newspapers, recreation, shopping, transportation, and more for the city you are moving to, and the same kinds of information about the state, plus regulations governing bringing cars, guns, pets, plants, and other items into the state.

Some movers will also, using your information, prepare an individual cost-of-living analysis for your family, comparing your old cost of living to your projected cost of living in the new town.

Ask your mover what information services are available and the cost of those services.

Commonly Asked Questions

Q. *I am being transferred in three months and don't know anything about the town we are moving to. How can I learn about it?*

A. Write or call the chamber of commerce in the new town and ask for a newcomer's package. Subscribe to the local newspaper. Look at books about the area. Go online and search for information.

CHAPTER 3

Estimating Moving Costs

What is it going to cost you to move? You have a lot of control over the bottom line. You can keep costs at rock bottom by borrowing equipment, calling on friends, and doing most of the work yourself. Or you can let a moving company do it all while you concentrate on your new job and settling into your new home. Most moves will fall somewhere in the middle.

With a bit of calculating, you can make a pretty good estimate on the total cost of the move. Even if you hire a moving company, your moving costs include more than just their bill. You may have travel costs, storage, shipment of special belongings, shipment of pets, and other expenses, many of which are tax deductible.

Depending on your point of view, you may consider other expenses a part of the move. Those could include deposits on utilities, membership dues, paint for sprucing up your old house, and even remodeling. None of those are tax deductible as moving expenses, however. They generally come under the category of home purchase expenses.

For current, accurate guidelines on moving expenses, consult either your own accountant or tax expert or the Internal Revenue Service.

Estimating the Cost of Using a Moving Company

Your moving company will give you an estimate of their cost. Be sure that you understand the estimate. You need to know what kind of estimate it is—whether binding or non-binding—and you need to know exactly what services will be performed for the price.

Your mover will probably charge you for a *binding* estimate because it means that you and the moving company agree on a total price before the move. You cannot be charged more unless additional services are required. The mover cannot charge you for a nonbinding estimate, which is less accurate than a binding estimate. A *nonbinding* estimate allows the mover to later bill on the actual weight of the shipment and services performed. If the shipment is local, the estimate may be based on hourly charges.

Know exactly what services will be performed by the moving company under the conditions of the estimate. Does the estimate include packing? Preparing appliances? Disassembly of certain items? Will they take things off the walls or must you have that done before the movers arrive?

The topic of moving company estimates is covered thoroughly in Chapter 5.

Estimating the Cost of a Do-It-Yourself Move

Estimating the cost of a do-it-yourself move is actually pretty easy, too. You need to determine the size of the truck or trailer and any other equipment, such as dollies, furniture pads, tow bar, or automobile transport you will rent. You need to estimate how much packing material (boxes, tape, rope) you need. You also must figure out the cost of labor to help you pack and load.

☞ **Money-$aving Tip #5** *Estimating the cost of moving with the help of a moving company and estimating the cost of moving yourself will help you determine what kind of move best fits your budget.*

Rental Vehicle Cost

Probably the biggest expense of your move will be the charge for renting the truck or trailer. Chapter 6 includes some guidelines for deciding how large a truck or trailer you need to hold your belongings. Your truck rental agent will also help you determine your needs.

While it may be tempting to try to save money on the rental of the truck by using a small vehicle and a cut-rate rental agency, be wary of trying to save in such ways. If you rent a small truck and then can't get everything into it, you have three choices. First, you can try to switch with the rental company for a larger truck, but who wants to unload and reload that whole truckful? Second, you can make two trips if your move is short. This, however, may end up costing more because of fuel. Your time is valuable, too. Two small loads take more time than one large load. Third, you can leave some things behind—probably not a good choice, either.

Using a cut-rate truck rental company is also risky. Is the truck you will drive in good repair? What happens if it breaks down ten miles outside your new hometown? Does it have air-conditioning for your summer trip? Is the cab clean and comfortable?

☞ **Money-$aving Tip #6** *Avoid false economy in your move. Using cut-rate equipment and materials can end up costing more in the long run. Deal only with reputable companies with dependable equipment.*

When you rent the truck, you will also want to rent a utility dolly. The few dollars for the rental is money well spent because the dolly will make the loading job much easier and quicker. If you are loading appliances, you may want to rent an appliance dolly also. Furniture pads will protect your furniture and appliances from scratches, dents, and gouges during the drive.

Remember that the cost of renting the truck does not include the cost of fuel or additional insurance. Fuel is a separate expense you will incur.

Moving Materials Costs

You can save money on packing materials, but experienced movers know how much better moving boxes and cartons are than grocery and liquor boxes. Moving boxes are sturdy and of uniform size, making them ideal for stacking. Special dish packs (see Figure 3.1), wardrobe cartons, mirror boxes, and others will keep your things safer during the move.

Newspaper is cheap and works for packing around things in boxes, but it is dirty. The ink will rub off on your hands and clothes as you work and on the things you pack it around. You can purchase clean wrapping paper instead. One option is to wrap your dishes in clean paper so they don't have to be rewashed, and then wrap other things in newsprint. You can also purchase bubble wrap and packing peanuts. If you know ahead of time that you will be moving, you can save such packing materials from items you purchase.

FIGURE 3.1 Boxes and cartons made specially for packing and moving keep your possessions safe during the move.

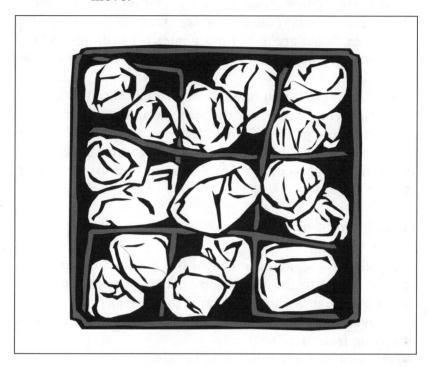

You will also need packaging tape and rope for tying off your load. Chapter 8 offers some guidelines on determining your packing materials needs. You can also ask your truck rental company for advice. Many suppliers will allow you to return any unused materials for a full refund.

Labor Costs

Who's going to do all that packing, lift and carry all those boxes, and move the furniture and appliances? If you don't have the people-power in your family to handle all those tasks, you will need to seek out either volunteer or paid helpers.

If you need to hire help, remember that a small, efficient crew will work better than a large, disorganized group. Ask around. Your truck rental agent may know of some unemployed movers who could use a day job. Check with moving companies. What are their hourly rates for loading? Call the local employment office. They may have a list of day laborers.

How much will you have to pay? What about insurance for day laborers? Again, ask the same people. Pay a fair wage and you should get good work. If boxes are packed and the household prepared for moving, two or three men can load a large truck in less than a day. Estimate your cost from that.

Travel Costs of Moving

Somehow, you and the rest of the family must get from the old house to the new house. This is inexpensive and easy if the move is within the same town or city. The further the move, however, the more complex and costly the task of getting from here to there.

Let's look at some options and costs.

Airplane, Train, or Bus

If everything from the house, including your car, is being moved in a moving company van, you and the family might opt to fly or take a bus or train to the new town. Flying makes a quick transition, while the train or bus will allow the family to get a real sense of change.

The cost of any tickets are legitimate moving expenses.

Automobile

If you sent off your household goods in a moving company van, you can drive to the new house in your own car.

The gasoline or diesel fuel to transport you by automobile from the old house to the new is another legitimate moving expense. One advantage of driving to the new house is that you can set your own route and schedule, as long as you are on hand at the new house on delivery day.

If you don't know what kind of gas mileage your car gets, check a tank or two before your move. All you need to do is note the odometer reading when you fill up. Then, the next time you fill up, note the reading again. Subtract the beginning reading from the ending reading to learn how many miles you drove on that tank of fuel. Then divide that number by the number of gallons it took to fill the tank the second time. There you have the number of miles per gallon you drove your car. When you get an average, multiply it by the number of miles you will drive from your old home to the new one and you will have an approximation of how many gallons of fuel you will need for the trip. Multiply that by the average cost per gallon of fuel for an estimate of your fuel costs for the trip.

Your rental truck will need fuel, too. Ask the rental agent approximately how many miles per gallon the truck gets—loaded. Naturally, the truck will get better mileage unloaded, so the agent may try to slip that number in instead of the loaded average mileage. With an accurate mileage estimate, you can figure your estimated fuel cost just as you did for a car.

Lodging

Longer moves require overnight lodging along the way. Depending on your moving budget, your needs, and your wants, you may average $40 or $50 per night, or you may spend upward of $200 per night. For a rushed trip on a tight budget, you may opt for a quiet, no-frills night's sleep. To make the trip more pleasant, you may choose an upscale motel with pool, spa, and other amenities. Or you may decide to pamper yourself and your family with a luxury hotel and room service.

If you know your route and schedule, you can make reservations ahead of time and know exactly what your lodging for the trip will cost. If you use a major motel or hotel chain, you can probably make all your reservations with one toll-free call. Take that number with you on your trip, too, just in case you need to cancel a reservation along the way. Even if you don't know your final route and schedule, you can estimate lodging costs pretty closely by looking through a few motel, hotel, and travel brochures for the areas you will be passing through. Motel rates do vary widely.

☞ **Money-$aving Tip #7** *Use toll-free numbers to make travel reservations at motels or hotels along your travel route. Be sure to ask for the best rate. Senior-citizen rate? Business rate? Family rate? Sometimes just asking helps.*

Food

You all have to eat along the way. If your move will take less than a day's drive, you can get by with snacks in the car or a picnic at a rest area. Or you might treat the family to a lunch or dinner at a fancy restaurant before you reach your new home.

On a longer move, however, especially if you are driving the truck or traveling by car, you will want to establish a food budget. You already have a good idea what your family likes to eat. Do you all need three complete meals per day? Can you make a breakfast of granola bars and fruit? You might carry a cooler or ice chest filled with snacks, breakfast, and lunch foods, and stop for one full meal per day. Or you might eat a big, late lunch—usually cheaper than dinner menus—and finish the day with lighter fare such as a salad.

To estimate your food costs for the move, decide how you will eat, determine approximately what it will cost per day, and multiply that by the number of days you will be on the road.

☞ **Money-$aving Tip #8** *You can save on your food bill during a trip by carrying an ice chest and stopping at grocery stores rather than eating in restaurants three times a day. Buy fruits, granola bars, juice, even sandwich makings. You will eat more healthfully, feel better, and save money besides.*

Sightseeing, Attractions, and Entertainment

Although not tax deductible, fun while traveling to your new home may be within your moving budget. Everyone in the family has worked hard to get ready for the move. If your budget allows, give everyone the reward they've earned. Even if it is a small amount, figure in something for having fun.

Get a book on national parks and check entrance fees. They are usually very reasonable. Find toll-free numbers for major attractions along the way. How much is a one-day pass to Disney World? What would it cost to spend a few hours at a water park in a city on your travel route? Many cities offer sightseeing tours. You can usually see many of the major sights of the city in a few hours, at a reasonable cost, without getting lost. Or you can see the downtown area in a horse-drawn carriage. Look around. There's something fun to do almost anywhere.

And remember, there are lots of fun things you can do for free. Many parks are free. Lots of small museums only ask for a donation. Short side trips to see country lanes, fall colors, or spectacular waterfalls cost only a little fuel.

You all deserve a little fun in between the work of moving out and the work of moving in.

☞ **Money-$aving Tip #9** *If you are moving to another city or state, you can make the trip fun without adding significantly to your moving expenses. Visit state and national parks. Stop at historic sites. Detour for short scenic drives. Each state has fun, free or low-cost things to do.*

Other Moving Costs

There will be other costs to your move, some minor and some significant, depending on your situation. With a little forethought, you can anticipate most of these costs and include them in your budget.

Here are some common miscellaneous moving costs.

Storage

When you cannot move straight from the old house to the new house, you have to put all your belongings somewhere. This can happen when you have to move quickly and have not located a permanent home in the new town. Or it can happen when you find a new home, but cannot take possession (either rental or purchase) for a few days or even weeks after you have to be out of the old house. It can also happen when you purchase a house that needs remodeling. Sometimes the work cannot be completed or nearly enough completed for you to move in before you have to vacate your old home. And if you are building a home, unexpected delays seem to be the rule rather than the exception.

So, what do you do with all your things while you are staying in a motel, hotel, campground, or with friends?

If you only need to store your possessions for a very short time, they may even stay on the moving company truck for a few days if the truck is not needed elsewhere. Of course, there will be a storage charge for those days. It may be cheaper to keep a rental truck a couple days extra than to unload your things and rent a truck again. If you must leave your things stored in the truck, back it up to a wall if possible so that the back cannot be broken into.

For short-term storage (under 30 days), check with your mover or rental truck agency. Many offer short-term storage. Compare their rates with local self-storage units. At least one national rental truck firm advertises 30 days of free storage with one-way truck rental. Sounds like a good deal. Remember, if you are moving yourself, you will need to borrow or rent a truck a second time to move your goods from your storage site to your new house.

Here's one other alternative: If you are remodeling but it does not affect the garage or basement, you might be able to store all or at least most of your things there. If you are waiting for someone to move out of the house, you might work a deal with them to store your things in the garage or basement if they have already cleared out those areas.

Temporary storage costs are a tax-deductible moving expense.

☞ **Money-$aving Tip #10** *If you need to store your belongings between homes, check prices carefully. Learn the costs of storing your things with your mover, with your truck rental company, and in a self-store unit.*

Temporary Accommodations

Just as you may need a temporary home for your possessions, for all the same reasons you may need a temporary home for yourself and your family. If you own a motor home or travel trailer, you have an easy solution. Otherwise, you will have to find somewhere to stay until your new home is ready for occupancy.

Do you have relatives or good friends in the new town? They may offer you a place to stay, or at least may be able to make some suggestions about temporary lodging.

Some hotels and motels offer weekly or monthly rates. If you need this alternative, you can feel more at home if you find a room or rooms with kitchen facilities. Look for inexpensive suites of rooms so that each family member can have at least some privacy. Too much togetherness can strain relationships.

If you need longer-term temporary accommodations, look at apartments that rent on a month-to-month basis. Check the newspaper and local real estate agents.

It's easy to estimate your temporary accommodation costs if you know where you will stay and when your new home will be ready. Your estimate will be less exact if you don't know those two facts.

☞ **Money-$aving Tip #11** *If you must find temporary lodging between homes, check around for motels or hotels that offer weekly or monthly rates in addition to nightly rates. The savings can be significant. If you are staying for several days or more, you probably don't need clean linens every night or the room cleaned daily. Your room rate should drop accordingly.*

Insurance

Check into insurance coverage for your possessions that are being transported. Although most moves go without incident, accidents do happen, loads do shift and cause damage to the contents, and loss occurs.

Even if you ship your household goods with a professional moving company, you will probably want to purchase more than the basic insurance coverage that comes with your contract. It is unlikely that the basic insurance will adequately protect the value of your shipment. Ask your mover to explain the coverage offered, and read the information on insurance in Chapter 5.

If you are moving yourself, learn what insurance coverage the truck rental company provides. Check your homeowner and auto insurance policies also to learn whether either already covers you, your vehicles, any volunteer helpers, and your possessions in transit. If you do not already have coverage, you may be able to purchase a short-term policy or rider that will insure you adequately.

So, What Is It Going to Cost You to Move from Here to There?

Your moving budget and your final moving costs will be unique to your situation. The cost to you will be minimal if your employer is picking up the tab. The total may be quite high if you are letting a moving company move you and you are flying to the new location or taking a leisurely trip along the way. Your move will probably fall somewhere in the middle.

Your move may include expenses from some or all of the following categories. You may want to use this list to total your estimates.

- Moving company   _____
- Truck or trailer rental   _____
- Other equipment rental   _____
- Pack-and-stack service   _____
- Packing material (boxes, tape, rope, etc.)   _____
- Labor   _____
- Travel fares   _____
- Pet transport   _____
- Transport of delicate/special items   _____
- Disconnect/connect utilities   _____
- Appliance preparation for moving   _____
- Fuel   _____
- Travel lodging (hotel, motel, campground)   _____
- Food   _____
- Sightseeing/attractions/entertainment   _____
- Storage   _____
- Temporary accommodations   _____
- Insurance   _____
- Other   _____

Where you can cut moving costs. One way you can
cut moving costs drastically is to do more of the work yourself. A moving company will gladly take over and do everything from packing to unpacking. You just pay the bill. You
can cut that bill dramatically by doing your own packing or
most of your own packing. You may want to let the professionals pack your most treasured or valuable furnishings.

You can also cut costs by performing a do-it-yourself
move rather than hiring a moving company. If you want to
do the loading and driving, but not the majority of the packing, look into the services and costs of a pack-and-stack service in your area. They will pack all your boxes safely and
leave them stacked and ready to load onto the truck.

If you do it all, from packing to driving to unpacking, you
can move from your old house to your new house for approximately half the cost of letting a moving company do it
all. You can save even more if you are willing to scavenge
grocery and liquor stores for sturdy boxes to pack in. You
can also call a few moving companies to see if they will sell
you good, used packing boxes. Save newspapers for packing material.

Try to move during the off-season. Far more people move
in the summer. If you can move during the winter, try to
negotiate an off-season rate with your mover or truck rental
company. You can also take advantage of winter rates at motels along the way, as long as you avoid ski areas and winter
resorts.

If you are moving cross-country and driving, you can save
by making the drive as quickly as possible. Two drivers will
mean you can put in longer days on the road, saving a night
or two of motel bills. That also saves the cost of several restaurant meals, which can add up quickly.

Making your travel plans well ahead of time can also be a
money saver. If you are traveling by air, bus, or train,
research the best rates. Talk to your travel agent early to take
advantage of the best rates by purchasing tickets early. Or go

online with your computer and do your own checking. Sometimes purchasing round-trip tickets is more cost effective than one-way tickets. Don't overlook any possibilities.

☞ **Money-$aving Tip #12** *Negotiate with your current or new employer for coverage of moving costs. Even if they say company policy doesn't normally cover moving costs, give it a try. If your employer won't pay for a moving company to move you, maybe you can be reimbursed for moving yourself with a rental truck. Or maybe you can negotiate a set dollar amount toward your relocation expenses. Give your employer a chance to help!*

Moving Costs Are Tax Deductible

Keep a record of all your moving expenses. If your move meets certain criteria, you can deduct many moving expenses from your federal income taxes. Because federal tax laws change rapidly and are subject to interpretation, check with your tax adviser to make sure you deduct all legal moving expenses.

Following are the current criteria for eligibility for deduction:

1. You must move near to where you will work and you must move close to the time you start your new job. Moving expenses within a year from the time you begin work qualify, whether you had the job before you moved or not.

2. Your main job location for the new job must be at least 50 miles further from your old home than your old main job location.

3. If you are employed by someone else, you must work full-time for at least 39 weeks during the first year after arriving in the area of your new job. This does not all have to be for the same employer nor do

the 39 weeks have to be consecutive. If you file a joint return, either you or your spouse may meet this guideline.

What Expenses Are Deductible?

What can you deduct? Currently, if you meet the above requirements, you can deduct the most expensive parts of your move. Those include:

- Packing, crating, and loading your belongings
- Unloading, unpacking, and uncrating your belongings
- Shipping of your household goods
- Shipping of your personal automobile
- Transporting of your pets
- Travel expenses for the family (except meals)
- Temporary storage of household belongings (up to 30 days)

What Expenses Are Not Deductible?

Many of the costs associated with moving are not deductible. These include house-hunting trips, temporary accommodations, and closing costs of selling or purchasing a home. A more complete list of exclusions includes:

- House-hunting trips
- Temporary accommodations
- Closing costs of selling or purchasing a home
- Home improvements to help sell your home
- Purchase price of a new home
- Loss on the sale of your home
- Mortgage penalties
- Real estate taxes
- Losses from club/organization memberships
- Automobile and driver's license transfers

Again, be sure to check with your tax adviser for the most current information on what is deductible.

☞ **Money-$aving Tip #13** *Keep accurate records of all costs of your move. This information will be useful in budgeting and at tax time.*

How *Your Agent Can Help*

Your real estate agent can help you with the costliest part of your move—purchasing your new home. Your agent will help you get the best price for the home you are selling and also help you find an affordable home in your new location.

Your agent can also help you get in touch with people who can help reduce the cost of your move. Because agents work with people who are moving, they can usually provide a list of the moving companies and truck rental companies in the area, as well as other professionals who can provide services you need. By contacting them and comparing costs and services, you can hire the people who will do the best job for the least cost. Be sure to visit their offices and warehouses to see firsthand how your possessions will be treated while in their care.

If you need temporary housing in your new location, your agent can do some preliminary searching for you with affiliates in the new town, or at least put you in touch with a reliable agent there.

Commonly Asked Questions

Q. How much can I save by moving myself?

A. Truck rental companies estimate that you can save as much as 50 percent by renting and driving a truck yourself rather than hiring a moving company.

Q. How else can I save money if I don't want to do the driving myself?

A. You can hire a moving company to do the loading and driving, but pack everything yourself. Or you can find a shipping company that will deliver a van to your home for you to load, then will drive your goods to your destination.

Q. Is my move tax deductible?

A. If your move is work related and meets a few guidelines, it is tax deductible. The IRS or your tax adviser can give you the latest guidelines.

CHAPTER 4

Deciding How Much to Do Yourself

There's no way around it: Moving is a big job. One of your first tasks is to decide how much of the job you will do yourself. To decide how much to do yourself, you will want to evaluate your situation. This chapter will help you take a look at the factors affecting your decision so that you can make the best choice for you and your family.

First, you need to know how far you will be moving. You will need to decide what you will move and what you will leave behind. You will need to make an estimate of the weight or volume of your belongings. Then you will review your resources for moving: your budget, your health and physical condition, and the help and vehicles you have available. From this, you will determine how much of the job you want to do yourself, anywhere from moving it all yourself with your own or a borrowed truck or trailer, to having a moving company prepare and pack everything and unpack and prepare it at the other end.

Let's get started.

Evaluating the Situation

Even if you're lucky enough to have an employer footing the bill for your move, you may have to do a lot of the work yourself. Some employers will pay for the entire move, while others cover a portion, and still others will pay the cost of a do-it-yourself move. If your employer is paying for the move, the first thing you need to do is get clear on exactly what expenses will be covered. Some companies will pay for everything: packing, transporting, storing, and unloading; travel costs for the family; and temporary housing and meals during house-hunting in the new city.

Others will pay the cost of the rental truck and fuel only. Many fall somewhere in-between. As soon as you know how much your employer will be involved in planning and paying for the move, you can determine how much you and your family will do and how much you will hire to be done.

How Far You Have to Go

Some moves are just down the hall, from apartment to apartment. Some moves are from one country to another. Whether you are moving down the hall, across the river, or from Kentucky to Maine, it will take energy to get from here to there. There are boxes to pack, furniture to move, and the further you go, the more energy and investment it will take.

How far are you going?

Moving Across Town

Don't be lulled into thinking that a move across town is much easier than a move across the country. Many people mistakenly believe that a crosstown move can easily be accomplished in a day with one or two trucks. That is true only for college students and other young people just starting out who have few possessions. Using unstable, topless boxes from the grocery store and loading them into your car or pickup is also a good way to end up with many broken items. Even a short move requires that breakables be packed securely. Clothing thrown in boxes or on the seat, or even folded in a suitcase will probably need ironing, maybe even washing, upon arrival, while clothing packed in wardrobe boxes will arrive clean and still pressed.

You will probably be less likely to hire a moving company to move you across town than if your move is from Michigan to Louisiana. Rental truck and trailer companies offer a good compromise. Call at least two rental companies to get competitive bids. If you rent a trailer or truck, it is usually most cost and time effective to rent a unit large enough to haul everything in one load. You can purchase boxes and other packing materials from the rental company, and you can rent furniture dollies and furniture pads to protect your possessions. Even if you rent your truck or trailer, you can still hire help with packing and loading, unpacking and unloading. If you don't have enough strong young men in your family or circle of friends, ask around or call the local employment office for temporary by-the-hour help. Ask for someone with experience moving.

Moving Within Your Home State

Moving from one city to another within your home state will require somewhat more planning, preparation, and work than a crosstown move. For a crosstown move you may be able to borrow a truck or several trucks and get a bunch of friends and relatives to help for the price of several pizzas, sodas, and beer (no alcohol until all work and driving is done!). Few friends can offer to help when the move is several hundred miles, and the time and expense to return borrowed transportation may be more than the cost of a rental vehicle. Or, you may decide to hire a mover to ensure that everything arrives at your new home in top condition.

Moving Across the Country

Moving halfway or all the way across the United States is somewhat more difficult than moving across your home state and requires a few more decisions. While you may be comfortable piloting a large rental truck a few hundred miles on familiar highways, you may hesitate to take the responsibility for driving that same truck several days for 2,500 or 3,000 miles across long stretches of deserted highway, over mountain passes, through large cities, and down country lanes. The time of year may also dictate some decisions. While a spring trip over the Rockies may sound inviting, a midwinter blizzard could ruin all your plans. How will your personal vehicles arrive? Will you tow a car behind this unfamiliar truck? Will your spouse or a friend drive the car? What if you get separated?

If you move across one or more state boundaries, you may want to make the trip in your car to see the countryside. You can then relax and enjoy the trip. And your car can make many side trips and see many attractions and natural wonders that may not accommodate a truck.

Moving to Another Country

Unless all you plan to take to your new home in another country is your clothing and a few personal possessions, you will need a way of shipping your goods, whether you arrange it through an international shipper or a moving company. You can pack, box, and crate it all for a shipper, or you can let an international moving company do it all.

If you decide to do it all yourself, you will need to do all the research on how and what you can ship, knowing there are restrictions on the importation of certain goods into certain countries. If you hire a moving company, they should be able to furnish most of the information on this topic.

What You Have to Move

Some people only need to pack a suitcase or two and be ready to move next door, across the country, or halfway around the world. Other people require the largest moving van available (or even more). How much do you have to move? A room full? A house full? A whole farm full? How much of the physical work of moving you plan to do will depend a great deal on how much you have to move. Here are some hints on determining how much you have to move.

Take inventory of what you have to move (see Figure 4.1). Getting a rough estimate of the cubic feet (the standard measurement for moving) you have to move will help you decide if you want to carry and load it all yourself, or if you need to hire a mover, and will also help you determine the costs involved. Use the following chart to make a room-by-room inventory of the goods you need to move. A couple of hours making an inventory will help you enormously in your planning and budgeting.

A total of the cubic feet of these items will give you a good start on estimating the size of the moving load you will have. Remember, in addition to these large items, all decorative pieces, dishes and other kitchenware, personal items, books, clothing, bedding, memorabilia, and other items have to be packed and moved also. Should your household include pets, other hobbies, or a business, these will anywhere from slightly to greatly increase the load.

One truck rental company estimates that a one- or two-bedroom home of under 1,200 square feet will include about 35 boxes, a two- or three-bedroom home of 1,200 to 1,600 square feet will require about 50 boxes, a three- or four-bedroom home of 1,600 to 2,000 feet will need about 70 boxes, and a home larger than 2,000 square feet will fill about 120 boxes. That's a lot of wrapping, packing, and loading!

FIGURE 4.1 Room-by-Room Inventory Worksheet

Room/Item	Cubic feet	# pieces
Living Room		
Book shelves	5	_____
Bookcase	15	_____
Chair–arm	10	_____
Chair–recliner	20	_____
Chair–rocker	12	_____
Couch	30–40	_____
Desk	20–40	_____
Fireplace equip.	5	_____
Grandfather clock	20	_____
Lamp–floor	3	_____
Lamp–table	2	_____
Magazine rack	2	_____
Piano	50–70	_____
Stereo components	3	_____
Stereo console	20	_____
Table–coffee/end	4	_____
TV–console	15	_____
TV–portable	10	_____
_____	_____	_____
Kitchen/Dining Room		
Bar–portable	15	_____
Buffet	20–30	_____
Cabinet	20–30	_____
Chair	5	_____
China cabinet	25	_____
High chair	3	_____
Hutch	25	_____
Stool	3	_____
Table	10–20	_____
_____	_____	_____

FIGURE 4.1 Room-by-Room Inventory Worksheet (Continued)

Room/Item	Cubic feet	# pieces
Bedroom/Children's Room		
Bassinet	4	_____
Bed–king	75	_____
Bed–queen	55	_____
Bed–double	45	_____
Bed–single	30	_____
Bed–youth	20	_____
Bed–water	20	_____
Cedar chest	10–15	_____
Changing table	5	_____
Chair	4	_____
Chest/dresser	20–30	_____
Cradle	5	_____
Crib	10	_____
Night table	5	_____
Playpen	6	_____
Toy chest	5	_____
Wardrobe	35	_____
_____	_____	_____
Appliances		_____
Air conditioner	15	_____
Dishwasher	15	_____
Dehumidifier	10	_____
Clothes dryer	25	_____
Freezer	45–60	_____
Microwave	5	_____
Range	25	_____
Refrigerator	40	_____
Sewing machine	10	_____
Vacuum cleaner	5	_____
Washing machine	25	_____
_____	_____	_____

FIGURE 4.1 Room-by-Room Inventory Worksheet (Continued)

Room/Item	Cubic feet	# pieces
Office		
Bookcase	10–20	_____
Computer	5	_____
Filing cabinet	8	
_____	_____	_____
Garage/Outdoor Items		
Barbecue	5–10	
Bicycle	6	
Canoe	50	
Garden cart	5	
Golf bag	2	
Hose and tools	10	
Lawn chair	3	
Lawn mower	7	
Lawn swing/glider	20	
Picnic table	25	
Sandbox	10	
Stepladder	5	
Swing set	20	
Tool chest	3–10	
Tricycle	4	
Wagon	5	
Wheelbarrow	7	
_____	_____	_____

☞ **Money-$aving Tip #14** *Make a room-by-room inventory of the goods you need to move. A couple of hours making an inventory will help you enormously in your planning and budgeting.*

Your Moving Resources

When deciding how much of the move to do yourself (or with the help of family and friends), consider your moving resources. You should think about your budget, health, available help, time, vehicles, and moving knowledge and experience.

Let's consider your budget first, because it is often a deciding factor in how much you have to do.

Your Moving Budget

How much of the move you do yourself may be dictated by your budget. If you are on a shoestring, you will want to rustle up volunteer help and either borrow a truck or rent one for as short a time as possible. To really save every penny, you can contact local stores for sturdy boxes with lids, save newspaper for wrapping, whittle down your possessions, and rent the smallest truck you can stuff it all into. If you have more than you can take in your car or pickup, but not enough for a rental truck, check into renting a trailer or shipping your possessions with a commercial trucking company.

If you have a larger budget, you can purchase new or used cartons from your trucking or moving company, including specialized boxes for your wardrobe, mirrors, dishes, lamps, and other items. Renting furniture pads will help prevent scratches or gouges on your good wood or tears in upholstery. Skimping on good packing and loading materials is usually false economy. It's very disheartening to unload or unpack piece after piece of damaged or broken goods. Purchasing the appropriate boxes and cartons and packing them carefully yourself can save you dollars on the total bill.

Another option is for you to pack the majority of your boxes, leaving only the most breakable and most valuable possessions for the professionals to pack. Moving companies will not guarantee the safe arrival of boxes they do not pack unless there is obvious damage to the outside of the box.

If your budget stretches even further, you can have the moving company do all the packing, loading, unloading, placing, and unpacking. They will even move your vehicles and other large items. You can take off on your move and be assured that your goods will arrive on time and undamaged.

If your moving bill, or at least part of it, goes to your employer, you may still have several decisions to make. Your employer may pay for the loading and unloading of your possessions, leaving it to you to either pack yourself or pay to have the mover pack it all.

Talk to several moving companies about the variety of services they offer. Most of them are willing to do whatever part of the job you are not.

Health and Physical Condition

Moving a household full of heavy boxes, furniture, and appliances takes strength and stamina, even with the help of a utility dolly (see Figure 4.2). Even if you are in good health, are you in good shape? Make an honest appraisal of your physical abilities. Many people can carry lots of boxes and smaller items but are virtually useless for moving large furniture and appliances. You will need at least two people capable of lifting and carrying heavy items for several hours. Several people help divide the load, but too many create confusion. For packing a truck, some of the lifting will be overhead. If you are not in good physical condition as well as in good health, a sudden day of strenuous activity can leave you sore and tired, and even worse.

FIGURE 4.2 Moving is hard work. Be sure you are up to it physically before you decide to do it yourself.

Help

How much help do you have available? One or two people can do all the packing for the entire family, but more help will definitely lighten the load on moving day. As you announce your move to friends, family, and neighbors, several may offer to help. Take some of them up on it! It will be less tiring, make the task go more quickly, and be more fun. Will you have help available on both ends of the move? If your move is to a faraway city, you may have volunteers for the moving out, but be on your own for the moving in, although new neighbors and coworkers might pitch in. When Robert and Cheryl moved to their current hometown, a crew of several men from Cheryl's new employer showed up to help unload the rental truck. They were very welcome! Later, when Bob and Cheryl moved from a rental house to their new home, Cheryl posted a sign on the personal bulletin board at work and another crew showed up to help with that move.

If you don't get enough volunteers and you have teenagers, hire a couple of their friends. Or hire someone from your church who is temporarily unemployed. The local employment office may be able to send help at a reasonable wage. Be sure to supply water and other cold drinks during the day, and reward any volunteer help with a pizza or hamburger feed at the end of the day.

☞ **Money-$aving Tip #15** *You can save time and money by recruiting a volunteer crew to help with your move. You can save a significant amount, even if you use a moving company, if you and your family or a few friends do the packing.*

Time

If you accept a new job and have just a week before you show up for your first day at work, you will probably need to hire out more of the moving task than if you have two months' notice before moving. The more time you have, the more money you can save by doing it yourself. No matter how much time you have, the first step is to plan your move. In fact, the less time you have, the more important it is that you plan an efficient move. The moving calendar and notebook described in Chapter 7 will be critical in a quick move. The calendar will look crammed with tasks, but writing them down will help keep your mind clear, and crossing them off as they are accomplished will show you how much really is being done.

If you have plenty of time before you move, you can de-clutter, pack, load the van, clean the old house, travel to the new house, clean the new house, unload, unpack, and settle in with little help if that is what your budget requires or how you like to work. The shorter the lead time before moving, the more you will probably pay to have done.

Vehicles

It's difficult to move on a motorcycle or in a small car. If you have a large pickup or other roomy vehicle, however, you have more options. A move within the same town or even to a nearby town can be accomplished in one or more pickups, but it will take many hours, or even days, longer. If your budget is really tight and you or your friends don't have a truck or trailer, you may have to invest the extra time. Don't forget the cost of fuel for all the extra trips, though.

If you don't have an appropriate vehicle available but need to keep moving costs at an absolute minimum, you can rent a trailer or a small truck from a local truck rental dealer. One-day rental with return to the location where you rented is the least expensive. Again, remember to compute the cost of fuel for extra trips. It may be wise to rent a larger unit and do the entire move in one or two trips.

☞ **Money-$aving Tip #16** *If you don't have a truck or trailer of your own, renting a trailer is the most economical way to move your household goods. Remember that you will need a vehicle capable of towing whatever trailer you use.*

Moving Experience and Knowledge

How much experience do you have in packing breakables and in loading a truck? You or at least one of your helpers or paid workers should have some knowledge or experience.

If you do not, pay particular attention to the chapters in this book on packing and loading. Careful packing and loading can ensure that your possessions will arrive in good shape. In addition, the weight distribution in the trailer or truck can make driving easier or more dangerous.

Moving some household possessions may require special handling. If you plan to move a piano, much depends on the size, type, and value of the instrument. With care and a four-wheel dolly, you may feel confident in moving a full-size piano of modest value. Place a heavy piano at the front of the truck. If your piano is valuable, you may be well advised to let the experts prepare and move it to minimize the risk of damage.

Other

Doing a little research can help you plan and execute a move that is tailor-made for your family. Contact local truck rental companies for cost estimates. Have several moving companies assess your household and give you bids. Check other trucking companies for simple shipping of your goods. Many trucking companies will deliver a trailer to your home for you to load. They will then pick up the trailer, lock it, deliver it to your new home for you to unload, and pick up the empty trailer when you are finished. Check your phone book. Talk to people who have moved recently. Ask your real estate agent for information. Go online with your computer and search for moving and trucking companies.

Moving Options

Once you have evaluated all the above criteria, you will be ready to decide how much of the work to do yourself and how much to leave to the professionals. All you have left to do is to consider what services movers offer and how that fits into what you need. Here are the options.

Let the Mover Do It All

If you have a healthy budget or your employer is paying for the move, you can sit back and let the movers do it all. Even then, however, you might want to take the opportunity to sift through your belongings and eliminate what does not need to be moved. Better to do it now and not have to find places for it at the new house. And you will probably still be responsible for cleaning the home you leave and preparing the one you move into. You will also have to let all the appropriate people know you are moving, and arrange for transfer of school and medical records, banking, and other essentials. And it will be your task to settle everything at your new home once the movers unpack and leave. But the movers will do all the heavy work, from packing dishes, clothing, and breakables, to loading and unloading furniture and appliances.

Share the Job with a Moving Company

Many moves fall into this category. You may do everything up until the truck pulls up and the movers begin loading boxes and furniture onto the truck. This will save many dollars off the total moving bill and yet save you from the heaviest work.

It will also free you, if your move is out of town, to enjoy the trip to your new home. Some families like to take a leisurely drive to the new home, seeing a new part of the country and visiting historical sites and attractions along the way.

Do It All Yourself

If your budget is very limited or you are very independent, you may want to do it all yourself with your own, borrowed, or rented equipment and labor. One truck rental company claims that 75 percent of all moves are do-it-yourself jobs. You will save one-third to one-half the cost of a moving company move. And you will have complete control over all your possessions at all times. That also means you will have complete responsibility for your possessions and their safe arrival at the new house.

Are you a do-it-yourselfer?

How Your Mover Can Help

At this point, you probably have not yet chosen a moving company, but they will still offer you plenty of help. If you don't yet know how much of the job you will do yourself, get cost estimates from at least two truck rental companies and four moving companies. You can't make informed decisions without gathering the facts. Costs vary greatly depending upon services, equipment, reputation, season, distance, and other factors. Find out exactly what you get from each company. Moving services differ among companies.

Some companies will furnish maps, destination information, hints on moving, and other useful information. Several movers provide worksheets for getting a rough idea of the weight and cubic footage of your possessions, inventory sheets, moving calendars, and other aids. Accept all the literature you can get; you can always get rid of everything but the most helpful later.

If you have access to the Internet, go online and search for moving companies and truck rental companies. Many have Web sites with information you can download, and some offer online assistance and cost estimates through e-mail. See Chapter 11 for more details.

Commonly Asked Questions

Q. Why should I make an inventory of the contents of my home?

A. You will want to make an inventory of the contents of your home for three reasons. First, the inventory will help in determining what to move. As you list your inventory, mentally move each item into your new home. Does it fit? Can you replace it inexpensively? Consider the consequences of selling or giving away each item. Second, an inventory will help you estimate the cost of moving. If you are renting a trailer or truck, each item will take up space, increasing the cost of moving. If you are hiring a mover, each item will add weight, which will add to the final bill. Third, an inventory will allow you to check the load when you arrive at your destination. Is everything there? Is anything damaged? The inventory might even help you plan ahead where each appliance and piece of furniture will be placed in the new house.

Q. What do I have to move that is not on my inventory?

A. Hobby items, collections, special-interest items, and home-business equipment may not show up on your inventory. Do you have a model railroad system in your basement? Do you collect dolls from around the world? Do you have a library of hundreds of volumes? Do you make whirligigs in your garage to sell at craft fairs? These types of items, as well as kitchenware, personal items, and other items that require boxing, do not show up on the inventory lists in this chapter, but they take space and weight and must be considered in the cost of your move.

Q. How many boxes will I need to move my belongings?

A. Figure 35 boxes for a one-bedroom home, 50 boxes for a two- or three-bedroom home, 70 boxes for a three- or four-bedroom home, and 120 boxes for a larger home. That's a lot of packing!

Q. I have a pickup truck. Why not move with that?

A. You can move with a pickup. However, be aware that it will take many trips to move even a small household, so it is not feasible to move any distance in a pickup. Remember to figure the cost of fuel for all the trips and be aware that your time and the time of your helpers is valuable. If you are tempted to move in a pickup, do at least learn the costs of renting a larger trailer or truck. It just may be less than you expect for a local one-day move.

Q. How much will the movers do?

A. The movers will do nearly anything you ask them to, from packing at the old house through unpacking at the new house. There are a few items they will not handle for insurance purposes.

CHAPTER 5

Hiring and Managing a Mover

Hiring a professional moving company, whether they do everything from packing to unpacking, or simply picking up your prepared goods and transporting them to your new home, will greatly reduce the stress and the work that you invest in your move. Even if you expect to do it all yourself, you will be able to make a more informed decision if you get estimates from some moving companies. Then, if you do the move yourself, you will know just how much you saved. Or you may even decide that the extra expense is justified by simplifying your family's move.

Why Hire a Moving Company?

Sure, you can do it all yourself, with some help from friends, relatives, and neighbors. So why even think about hiring a professional mover? Because they are *professionals.*

FIGURE 5.1 A professional moving company will use the best packing materials to protect your belongings.

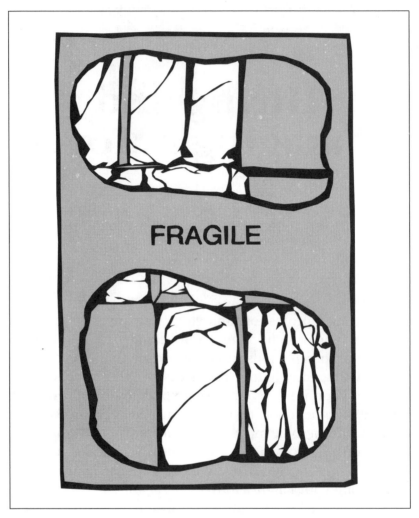

FRAGILE

That's why. Moving company employees have training and experience at their jobs. They have the supplies and equipment to pack and load your possessions safely and quickly. They use specially designed boxes for many items, such as dishes, electronics, clothing, and lamps (see Figure 5.1). They have the experience to complete the job quickly and efficiently. They are on the moving company's payroll and will take the job seriously. Your volunteer crew just might get distracted and begin an impromptu game of touch football on the front lawn!

Hiring a moving company also frees you to focus on other aspects of the move that sometimes get neglected if you have to do all the physical labor of packing and loading. If you hire a mover, you can help the kids through the emotional trauma of moving day. You will have more time to make sure the old house is left clean and the new one is ready to move into. And you can prepare more fully for your first day at the new job.

They Will Do It All for You

That's not really true, but moving company employees will do all the heavy work, from packing and loading to unloading and unpacking. And you can watch your houseful of possessions pull away from the old house knowing that everything is being done professionally, from the driving to the handling of your things to keeping track of where everything is. You will still have to handle all the tasks up until time for packing, make dozens of decisions, be on hand to answer questions during loading and unloading, and settle into your new home.

Also, there are a few items that moving companies cannot or will not transport. Your mover will most likely ask that you keep your valuable jewelry, furs, convertible documents (checks, stocks, etc.), insurance policies, and cash with you. And they will give you a complete list of other items they cannot carry.

If You Want to Pack It Yourself

You can save money by packing some or all of your possessions yourself. If you choose to do so, you can purchase all the specialty cartons you need directly from your mover. They will protect your goods much more effectively than liquor store or grocery store boxes. Another choice is to pack most of your things yourself, but leave the most valuable and most breakable for the professional packers. That way you will still save money, but chances are greater that everything will arrive at the new house in the same condition it left the old home.

If you decide to pack some or all of your things yourself, be sure to follow the packing directions in Chapter 8. If you run into trouble or run out of time, you can probably arrange for your mover to come to your home and pack what you haven't gotten to. Before you decide to do your own packing, find out from your mover how it will affect your insurance coverage. It may be that your mover will only guarantee safe arrival of items their professional packers handle.

What Your Moving Company Will Not Transport

Your mover should provide a list of items that are dangerous to transport. In fact, be sure you carefully read all the information they provide, especially the contract, because insurance coverage may be affected if you ship dangerous items. Your possessions will be closed in the back of the van where heat may become intense, so potentially explosive or flammable products cannot be included.

Aerosol cans of hair spray, shaving cream, cleaning products, paint, and garden and yard chemicals should not be packed. Nor should other flammables such as gasoline, ammunition, auto batteries, oil-based paints and paint thinners, bleach, matches, and other similar products. It is best not to transport such items in your car either for the same reasons.

Even in mild weather on a sunny day, the temperature in a closed car can exceed safe levels. The replacement of these few items is far more sensible than risking moving them any long distance.

Gas-powered engines such as lawn mowers should be emptied of oil and gasoline. Gas cans should be washed out. If your car is being transported, its gas tank should be no more than a quarter full. You may leave the oil at normal level.

While plants can legally be moved from some states, most movers will only move them at your own risk, with no insurance coverage.

Most movers also will not or cannot transport frozen foods.

When You Need to Store It

If the timing of your move is not just right, you may need to store your household goods for a few weeks while you find a new home in your new city, or while you wait for the one you have chosen to become available. Or you may want to remodel the house you have purchased, or even to build a new home on the perfect lot or five acres a few miles out of town.

While there are many places you can store your goods, including self-service storage units in many areas, it may be easiest to store your things with your moving company. If you think you will need storage, be sure to determine whether it is one of the services potential movers offer. An advantage of storing with your mover is that they will then deliver your furniture and other things when you are ready for them. And as with a self-service unit, you will probably be able to go to the warehouse and find things if necessary.

How to Choose a Moving Company

There are lots of moving companies out there willing to move your things and take your check. They are not all equal. Some are big with well-known names. You see their trucks on the highways daily and even parked down the block occasionally. Some are small and lesser known. How do you know which company to trust with all your worldly goods? You will have to do some research.

Ask friends, neighbors, relatives, coworkers, and anyone else you can think of to recommend a mover. Ask your real estate agent. Call at least six (eight is better) movers. At this point, you simply want to narrow the field down to three or four to ask for specific estimates so your questions will at first be more general than when you request an estimate. Are they certified? Certification means the company holds a certificate issued by the Interstate Commerce Commission (ICC) that allows them to move household goods between states. Are they available when you need to move? How long have they been in business? How much experience do their packers and drivers have? Do they offer storage? Are they licensed for interstate transport? Eliminate any company that is not helpful and willing to answer all your questions.

Now you can easily choose the three or four companies that impressed you the most and ask them for specific estimates. Because you are moving all your possessions, they should be willing, even eager, to send a company representative to your home to ask lots of questions, evaluate your household, and give you an estimate of the cost of moving from here to there. To get an accurate estimate, you will have to tell them exactly what is to be moved. You should now ask them lots of specific questions. Some suggested questions follow. You will have other questions depending on your situation.

- What services do you offer?
- What insurance coverage do you offer?

- Can I pack some or all of my own possessions?
- What guarantee do you offer that my goods will arrive in good condition?
- What is covered if I pack some of it myself?
- Do you supply packing materials? At what cost?
- Can you move my second car? My boat?
- Will you arrive on time to begin my packing and/or loading?
- Do you guarantee my things will arrive at my new home on the day we agree upon?
- Do you offer any discounts for senior citizens, the company I'm employed by, or off-season moves?
- Can I visit your office and see your equipment and local storage facility?
- Can I call you during the move and learn just where my things are at any given time?

You will probably have to wait until the moving company representative returns to the office and computes all the information before getting a price quote. Once you have the three or four estimates, you can decide on a mover. Price should not be the only factor you consider. Which company made you feel they would take the best care of your belongings? Which offers the services you need? If one estimate is much lower than the others, ask yourself why that might be. Did they forget to include something in the estimate? Unless you have a guaranteed price, you might be unpleasantly surprised at the discrepancy between their estimate and your final bill. If it sounds like a lot of work to select the best mover, just remember that they will be in charge of moving all the things that you cherish either across town or across the country. It's worth a little research and decision making to find the best mover for you.

☞ **Money-$aving Tip #17** *Choose your moving company carefully. Get at least four estimates and compare services, costs, reputation, and customer satisfaction.*

Mistakes to Avoid in Choosing a Mover

Experts in the moving industry point out the following mistakes to avoid when you are choosing your mover:

- Assuming that you cannot afford a mover without gathering any estimates
- Getting an estimate from just one moving company
- Not understanding the different types of estimates offered by movers
- Considering price only
- Not checking out the mover's reputation (Ask for references and check them out. Call the Better Business Bureau to check on complaints about the company.)
- Not clarifying any questions you have on the mover's liability and insurance
- Not understanding the bill of lading, which is the contract between you and the mover
- Not asking to meet some of the crew who will be handling your possessions

Your Rights and Responsibilities

When you move from one state to another, ICC regulations protect you and define your rights and responsibilities and those of your mover. Your mover is required to furnish you with a copy of an ICC pamphlet called *Your Rights and Responsibilities When You Move,* which tells you what those rights and responsibilities are. The following sections outline that information.

Binding and Nonbinding Estimates

A binding estimate holds the shipper to the estimate given to you, the consumer. You cannot be required to pay more than the amount of the estimate. A mover may charge for giving a binding estimate, which describes the goods to be shipped and the services to be provided. A binding estimate must be in writing and you must have a copy before you move. If you receive a binding estimate, you must pay by cash, certified check, or money order at the time of delivery unless the shipper agrees to other arrangements. If the charges are not paid at the time of delivery, the mover may hold your goods, with storage charges, until the bill is paid in full.

A nonbinding estimate does not bind the mover, nor is the mover permitted to charge for giving this estimate. A nonbinding estimate does not guarantee that the final cost will not exceed the estimate.

Nonbinding estimates must also be in writing and describe the shipment and all services provided. The estimate must be entered on the order for service and bill of lading relating to your shipment. If you are given a nonbinding estimate, do not sign or accept the order for service or bill of lading unless the estimate is entered on each form.

If you accept a nonbinding estimate, the mover cannot require you to pay more than the amount of the original estimate plus 10 percent *at the time of delivery.* You will then have at least 30 days after delivery to pay any remaining charges.

However, if you request the mover to provide more services than those included in the estimate, the mover may demand full payment for those added services at the time of delivery.

☞ **Money-$aving Tip #18** *A binding estimate holds the shipper to the estimate given to you, the consumer. You cannot be required to pay more than the amount of the estimate. A nonbinding estimate does not bind the mover, nor is the mover permitted to charge for one. When you receive a nonbinding estimate, there is no guarantee that the final cost will not exceed the estimate.*

Order for Service

You should also receive a copy of your mover's order for service. This is not a contract. Should your move be canceled or delayed or if you decide not to use the services of that mover, you should promptly cancel the order.

Should there be any change in the dates of pickup or delivery, or in the nonbinding estimate, the mover may prepare a written change to the order for service. That change should be attached to the order for service.

Bill of Lading Contract

The bill of lading is the contract between you and the mover. The mover is required by law to prepare a bill of lading for every shipment it transports. The information on the bill of lading must be the same information shown on the order for service. The driver who loads your shipment must give you a copy of the bill of lading before loading your furniture. You must also sign the bill of lading.

It is your responsibility to read the bill of lading before you sign it. If you do not agree with something on the bill of lading, do not sign it until you are satisfied that the bill of lading shows what service you want.

The bill of lading requires the mover to provide the service you have requested, and you must pay the mover the charges for the service. Be careful not to lose or misplace your copy of the bill of lading in the confusion of moving. Have it available until your shipment is delivered, all charges are paid, and all claims, if any, are settled.

Inventory

Although not required to do so, your mover's driver will probably inventory your shipment, listing any damage or unusual wear. The purpose of this is to make a record of the condition of each item. If the driver does not make an inventory, you should make one yourself.

After completing the inventory, the driver will usually sign each page and ask you to sign each page. Before you sign, make sure that every item in your shipment is listed and that the entries regarding the condition of each item are correct. You have the right to note any disagreement. Don't let anyone rush you through this task. When your shipment is delivered, if an item is missing or damaged, your ability to recover from the mover for any loss or damage may depend on the notations made on the inventory.

The driver will give you a copy of the full inventory. Attach it to your copy of the bill of lading—it is your receipt for the goods.

When your shipment is delivered, you are responsible for checking the items delivered against the items listed on your inventory. The driver usually places a small numbered tag on each item as the inventory is prepared. The tag numbers should correspond to the numbered items on the inventory form and facilitate checking off the items as they are brought into your new residence. Check each item for damage that did not exist when the shipment was loaded. If new damage is discovered, make a record of it in the space provided on the inventory form. Be sure to call the damage to the driver's attention and request that a record of the damage be made on the driver's copy of the inventory. If there is anything on the inventory that you do not understand, such as codes, don't hesitate to ask. Your right to make a damage claim later depends on this inventory. Check it thoroughly.

After the complete shipment is unloaded, the driver will request that you sign his copy of the inventory to show that you received the items listed. Do not sign the inventory until you have assured yourself that it is accurate and that proper notations have been entered on the form regarding any missing or damaged items. When you sign the inventory at the time of unloading, you are giving the driver a receipt for your goods.

☞ **Money-$aving Tip #19** *Read the bill of lading and inventory sheets carefully. The bill of lading is your contract. The inventory is your record of your possessions and their condition. You will need these papers if there are any questions about your shipment after delivery.*

Shipments Subject to Minimum Weight or Volume Charges

Movers usually have a minimum weight or volume charge for transporting a shipment. Usually the minimum is the charge for transporting a shipment of at least 500 pounds.

If your shipment appears to weigh less than the mover's minimum weight, the mover is required to advise you on the order for service of the minimum cost before agreeing to transport the shipment. Should the mover fail to advise you of the minimum charges and your shipment is less than the minimum weight, the final charges must be based on the actual weight instead of the minimum weight.

Determining the Weight of Your Shipment

If charges are to be based upon the weight of the shipment, the mover is required to weigh the shipment. Unless your shipment weighs less than 1,000 pounds and can be weighed on a warehouse platform scale, the mover is required to determine the weight of your shipment by one of the following processes.

Origin weighing—If your shipment is weighed in the city or area from which you are moving, the driver is required to weigh the truck on which the shipment is to be transported before coming to your residence. This is called the tare weight. At the time of this first weighing, the truck may already be partially loaded with one or more other shipments. This will not affect the weight of your shipment. The truck should also contain pads, dollies, hand trucks, ramps, and other equipment normally used in the transportation of household-goods shipments.

After loading of your possessions, the truck will be weighed again to obtain the loaded weight, called the gross weight. The net weight of your shipment is then obtained by subtracting the tare weight from the gross weight.

Destination weighing—The mover is also permitted to determine the weight of your shipment at the destination, the time of unloading. The fact that a shipment is weighed at the destination instead of at the origin will not affect the accuracy of the weight of your shipment. The most important difference is that the mover will not be able to determine the exact cost for your shipment until it is unloaded.

Destination weighing is done in reverse to origin weighing. After arriving in the city or area to which you are moving but before coming to your new residence to unload, the driver will weigh the truck, with your shipment still loaded on it, to obtain the gross weight. After unloading you shipment, the driver will again weigh the truck to obtain the tare weight. The weight of your shipment will then be obtained by subtracting the tare weight from the gross weight.

Each time a weighing is performed, the driver is required to obtain a weight ticket showing the date and place of weighing and the weight obtained. The ticket must also have your name and shipment number entered on it, along with the identification numbers of the truck. The ticket must be signed by the person who performed the weighing. If both the empty (tare) and loaded (gross) weighings are performed on the same scale, the record of both weighings may be entered on one weight ticket.

At the time the mover gives you the freight bill to collect the charges, a copy of every weight ticket relating to your shipment must accompany your copy of the freight bill.

You have the right to observe every weighing. The mover is required to inform you of the specific location of each scale that will be used and to allow you a reasonable opportunity to be present. If you desire to observe either or both of the weighings, you should tell the mover at the time the order for service is prepared or, in any event, before the day of your move. This will enable the mover to contact you before the weighing to advise you of the location of the scale(s).

Reweighing of Shipments

If your shipment is weighed at origin and you agree with the mover that you will pay the charges at time of delivery, the mover is required to give you written notice of the weight and charges on your shipment before unloading at your destination residence. If you believe that the weight is not accurate, you have the right to request that the shipment be reweighed before unloading.

The mover is not permitted to charge for the reweighing. If the weight of your shipment at the time of the reweigh is different from the weight determined at origin, the mover must recompute the charges based on the *reweigh* weight.

Before requesting a reweigh, you may find it to your advantage to estimate the weight of your shipment using the following method:

1. Count the number of items in your shipment. Usually there will be either 30 or 40 items listed on each page of the inventory. For example, if there are 30 items per page and your inventory consists of four complete pages and a fifth page with 15 items listed, the total number of items will be 135. If an automobile is listed on the inventory, do not include that item in the count of the total items.

2. Subtract the weight of any automobile included in your shipment from the total weight of the shipment.

If the automobile was not weighed separately, its weight can be found on its title or license receipt.

3. Divide the number of items in your shipment into the weight. If the average weight is between 35 and 45 pounds per article, it is unlikely that a reweigh will prove beneficial to you and could result in your payment of *higher* charges. For example, if your 10,000-pound shipment includes 250 items, the average weight per item is 40 pounds, well within the normal range.

Experience has shown that the average shipment of household goods will weigh about 40 pounds per item. If a shipment contains a large number of heavy items, such as cartons of books, boxes of tools, or heavier-than-average furniture, the average weight per item may be 45 pounds or more.

☞ **Money-$aving Tip #20** *Ask to have your shipment reweighed if you have any question about the mover's numbers. The mover cannot charge you extra for a reweighing. Your bill is prepared based on the weight of your shipment.*

Picking Up and Delivering Shipments on the Agreed Dates

Agree with your mover on set dates for shipment pickup and delivery. It is your responsibility to determine on what date, or between what dates, you need to have the shipment picked up and on what date or between what dates, you require delivery. It is the mover's responsibility to tell you if the service can be provided on or between those dates or, if not, on what other dates the service can be provided.

In the process of reaching an agreement with a mover, it may be necessary for you to alter your moving and travel plans if no mover can provide service on the specific dates you desire.

Do not agree to have your shipment picked up or delivered "as soon as possible." The dates or periods of time you and the mover agree on should be definite.

Once an agreement is reached on the dates service is to be provided, the mover is required to enter those dates on the order for service. Do not sign or accept an order for service that does not have the agreed dates for service entered on the form. Do not sign or accept an order for service that has dates for the pickup or delivery entered on it different from those dates to which you have agreed. The dates you have agreed upon must also be entered on the bill of lading and become part of your contract with the mover.

Once your goods are loaded, the mover is contractually bound to provide the service described in the bill of lading. The only defense for not providing the service on the dates called for in the contract is the "defense of *force majeure.*" This is a legal term meaning that if circumstances that could not have been foreseen and that are beyond the control of the mover prevent the performance of the service as agreed to in the bill of lading, the mover is not responsible for damages resulting from the nonperformance.

If, after an order for service is prepared, the mover is unable to make pickup or delivery on the agreed-upon dates, the mover is required to notify you by telephone, telegram, or in person about the delay. The mover must at that time tell you when your shipment can be picked up or delivered. If for any reason you are unable or unwilling to accept pickup or delivery on the dates named by the mover, you should attempt to reach agreement with the mover on an alternate date.

Agreeing on a delayed pickup or delivery date does not relieve the mover from liability for damages resulting from the failure to provide service as agreed. However, when you are notified of alternate delivery dates, it is your responsibility to be available to accept delivery on the dates specified. If you are not available and willing to accept delivery, the mover has the right to place your shipment in storage at *your* expense or hold the shipment on their truck and assess additional charges.

If after the pickup of your shipment, you request the mover to change the delivery date, most movers will agree to do so, providing your request will not result in unreasonable delay to their equipment or interfere with another customer's move. However, the mover is not *required* to consent to amended delivery dates and has the right to place your shipment in storage at *your* expense if you are unwilling or unable to accept delivery on the date agreed to in the bill of lading.

If the mover fails to pick up and deliver your shipment on the date entered on the bill of lading and you have expenses you otherwise would not have had, you may be able to recover those expenses from the mover. This is what is called an inconvenience or delay claim. Should a mover refuse to honor such a claim and you believe that you are entitled to be paid damages, you may sue the mover. The ICC has no authority, however, to order the mover to pay such items.

You should consider the possibility that your shipment could be delayed and, thus, find out before you contract with a mover to transport your shipment what payment you can expect if the service is delayed through the fault of the mover.

☞ **Money-$aving Tip #21** *Be sure that you are at the new house when the movers arrive to avoid any holding charges.*

Price and Service Options

It is customary for movers to offer price and service options.

The total cost of your move may be increased if you want additional or special services. Before you agree to have your shipment moved under a bill of lading providing special service, you should have a clear understanding with the mover what the additional cost will be. Remember that other movers may provide the service you require without charging additional fees.

One service option is a *space reservation.* If you agree to have your shipment transported under a space reservation agreement, you are required to pay for a minimum number of cubic feet of space in the moving van, regardless of how much space in the van is actually occupied by your shipment.

Another service option is *expedited service.* If you must have your shipment transported on or between specific dates and the mover could not ordinarily agree to do so in its normal operations, choose expedited service.

Another customary service option is *exclusive use of a vehicle.* If for any reason you desire or require that your shipment be moved by itself on the mover's truck or trailer, most movers will provide such service.

Still another service option is *guaranteed service* on or between agreed dates. If you take this service option, you enter into an agreement with the mover that provides for your shipment to be picked up, transported to the destination, and delivered on specific guaranteed dates. If the mover fails to provide the service as agreed, you are entitled to be compensated at a predetermined amount or a daily rate regardless of the expense you actually might have incurred as a result of the mover's failure to perform.

Before requesting or agreeing to any of these price and service options, be sure to ask the mover's representatives about the final costs you will be required to pay and consider all possible alternatives if you feel that the charges will be more than you are willing to pay.

Notification of Charges

You must advise the mover at the time you make the arrangements for the move if you wish to be notified of the weight or volume and charges on your shipment. You are required to give the mover a telephone number or address at which you will receive the notification.

The mover must notify you of the charges at least one 24-hour weekday prior to the delivery, unless the shipment is to be delivered the day after pickup. The 24-hour requirement does not apply when you obtain an estimate of the costs prior to the move or when the shipment is to be weighed at the destination.

Receipt for Delivery of the Shipment

At the time of delivery, the mover expects you to sign a receipt for your shipment. This is usually accomplished by having you sign each page of the mover's copy of the inventory.

Movers are prohibited from having you sign a receipt that relieves the mover from all liability for loss or damage to the shipment. Only sign receipts that indicate you are signing for your shipment in apparent good condition except as noted on the shipping documents.

The Mover's Liability for Loss or Damage

All moving companies are required to assume liability for the value of goods they transport. However, there are different levels of liability, and you should be aware of the amount of protection provided and the charges for each plan.

First, unless you make specific arrangements otherwise, the mover is required to assume liability for the entire shipment at an amount equal to $1.25 per pound times the weight of your shipment (ICC Plan). For example, if your shipment weighs 4,000 pounds, the mover will be liable to you for loss or damage up to $5,000. Although you have made no specific arrangements for this plan, the mover is entitled to charge you $7 for each $1,000 of liability. Under this arrangement, if you shipped a 10-pound painting valued at $1,000 in your 4,000-pound shipment, you could collect for the full value of the painting if it was lost or damaged. Under this plan, your valuables are somewhat protected, but you pay for it.

Next, if the value of your shipment exceeds $1.25 per pound, you may obtain additional liability protection from the mover. You do this by declaring a specific dollar value for your shipment. The amount you declare must exceed $1.25 per pound times the weight of the shipment. If you declare that your 4,000-pound shipment is worth $10,000, the mover will charge you $7 for each $1,000 of declared value, which in this case would result in a charge of $70. If you ship articles that are unusually expensive, such as art or antiques, be sure to declare their full value in the declaration of a specific amount. *You must do this in writing.*

Movers are permitted to limit their liability for loss or damage to "articles of extraordinary value," unless you specifically list other articles on the shipping papers. An article of extraordinary value is any item whose value exceeds $100 per pound. Your mover will provide you with a complete explanation of this limitation before you move. It is your responsibility to study this provision carefully and make the necessary declaration.

The least amount of liability a mover can assume when transporting your goods is called the "released value." Movers publish what are known as "released value rates." Under such rates, the mover assumes liability for not more than 60 cents per pound per article. Under this arrangement, if your 10-pound painting was lost or damaged and you had agreed to a released value shipment, the mover would be liable for not more than $6. Obviously, you should think carefully before consenting to such an agreement. There is no extra charge for this minimal protection, but you must sign a specific statement on the bill of lading agreeing to it. Remember that unless you do sign such an agreement, the mover is liable for $1.25 per pound, and can charge you for it.

Many movers offer their own added-value protection plans that differ in many respects from the ICC Plan. You should ask your mover for specific details of how their alternative plans operate and how much each costs before selecting the plan that is best for you.

The mover pays for loss or damage in each of the three forms of liability coverage described above. These are not insurance agreements. You have the additional option to agree to the released value transportation and obtain insurance directly from the moving company or from an insurance company.

Your mover can sell you or procure for you liability insurance in the amount you require if you release your shipment for transportation at a value of 60 cents per pound per article. In the event of loss or damage, which is the responsibility of the mover, the mover would be liable only for an amount not exceeding 60 cents per pound per article, and the balance of the loss would be recoverable from the insurance company up to the amount of insurance purchased. The mover's representative can advise you of the availability of such liability insurance and the cost per $1,000 of coverage.

If you purchase liability insurance from or through the mover, the mover is required to issue a policy or other written record of the purchase and provide you with a copy of the policy or other document at the time of purchase. If the mover fails to comply with this requirement, they become fully liable for any claim or loss or damage attributed to their negligence.

☞ **Money-$aving Tip #22** *Understand the insurance coverage provided by your mover. You will probably want to insure your goods for more than the minimum that automatically comes with shipment. That minimum amount will probably not cover costs should there be any damage or loss.*

Complaints and Inquiries about the Mover's Service

All movers are expected to respond promptly to complaints or inquiries from their customers. Should you have a complaint or question about your move, you should first attempt to obtain a satisfactory response from the mover's local agent, the sales representative who handled the arrangements for your move, or the driver assigned to your shipment.

If for any reason you are unable to obtain a satisfactory response from one of these persons, you should then contact the mover's principal office. When you make such a call, be sure you have at hand your copies of all the documents relating to the move. Particularly important is the number assigned to your shipment by the mover.

If you do not receive a satisfactory answer, you may contact the Interstate Commerce Commission's offices (see Appendix A for the regional office near you). Any time you contact the ICC regarding your shipment, you will need to furnish the name of the mover and the number assigned to your shipment.

All interstate moving companies are required to maintain a complaint and inquiry procedure to assist their customers. At the time you make the arrangements for your move, you should ask the mover's representative for a description of the mover's procedure, the telephone number to be used to contact the carrier, and whether the mover will pay for such telephone calls.

Payment of the Transportation Charges

At the time of payment of transportation charges, the mover must give you a freight bill identifying the service provided and the charge for each service. It is customary for most movers to use a copy of the bill of lading as a freight bill; however, some movers use an entirely separate document for this purpose.

Except in those instances where a shipment is moving on a binding estimate, the freight bill must specifically identify each service performed, the rate per unit for each service, and the total charges for each service. Do not accept or pay a freight bill that does not contain this information.

If your shipment was transported on a collect on delivery basis (COD), you will be expected to pay the total charges appearing on the freight bill at the time of delivery unless the mover provided a nonbinding estimate of approximate cost and the total charges for the services included in the estimate exceed 110 percent of the estimated charges.

It is customary for movers to provide in their tariffs that freight charges must be paid in cash, by certified check, or by money order. When this requirement exists, the mover will not accept personal checks. At the time you make arrangements for your move, you should ask the mover about acceptable forms of payment.

Some movers permit payment of freight charges by use of a credit card. However, do not assume that a nationally recognized credit card will be acceptable for payment. Ask the mover at the time the arrangements are made.

If you do not pay the transportation charges at the time of delivery, the mover has the right under the bill of lading to refuse to give you your goods. The mover may place them in storage at *your* expense until the charges are paid.

If, before payment of the transportation charges, you discover an error in the charges, you should attempt to correct the error with the driver, the mover's local agent, or by contacting the mover's main office. If an error is discovered after payment, you should write the mover (the address will be on the freight bill) to explain the error and request a refund.

Movers customarily check all shipment files and freight bills after a move has been completed to make sure the charges were accurate. If an overcharge is found, you will be notified and a refund made. If an undercharge occurred, you will be billed for the additional charges due.

Payment of Shipments Transported on Two or More Vehicles

Although all movers try to move each shipment in one truck, it becomes necessary at times to divide a shipment among two or more trucks. This frequently occurs when an automobile is included in the shipment and it is transported on a vehicle specially designed to transport automobiles. When this occurs, your transportation charges are the same as if the entire shipment moved on one truck.

If your shipment is divided for transportation on two or more trucks, you are not required to pay the total charges until all portions of the shipment have been delivered. However, as each portion of the shipment is delivered, the mover can require payment for that portion.

Movers are also permitted, but not required, to delay the collection of all the charges until the entire shipment is delivered. At the time you make the arrangements for your move, you should ask the mover about their policies in this respect.

☞ **Money-$aving Tip #23** *Be prepared to pay for your shipment as agreed, which is usually upon delivery. If you do not pay as agreed, the shipper can hold your shipment and charge storage.*

Payment of Shipments Lost or Destroyed in Transit

Movers customarily make every effort to assure that while your shipment is in their possession for transportation, no items are lost, damaged, or destroyed. However, despite the precautions taken, articles are sometimes lost or destroyed during the move.

In addition to any money you may recover from the mover to compensate for lost or destroyed articles, you are also entitled to recover the transportation charges represented by the portion of the shipment lost or destroyed.

On shipments with partial loss or destruction of goods, the transportation charges must be paid. The mover will return proportional freight charges at the time loss and damage claims are processed. Should your entire shipment be lost or destroyed while in the mover's possession, the mover cannot require you to pay any of the charges except the amount you have paid or agreed to pay for added liability protection. The fact that you do not pay any transportation charges does not affect any right you may have to recover reimbursement for the lost or destroyed articles, providing you pay the charges for added liability protection.

Filing Claims for Loss and Damage or Delay Dispute

Should your move result in the loss or damage to any of your property, you have the right to file a claim with the mover to recover money for such loss or damage.

You have nine months following either the date of delivery or the date on which the shipment should have been delivered to file a claim. However, you should file a claim as soon as possible. If you fail to file a claim within 120 days following delivery and later bring a legal action against the mover to recover the damages, you may not be able to recover your attorney fees even though you win the court action.

While the ICC maintains regulations governing the processing of loss and damage claims, it cannot resolve those claims. If you cannot settle a claim with the mover, you may file a civil action to recover in court. In this connection, you may obtain the name and address of the mover's agent for service of legal process in your state by contacting the applicable ICC regional office (see Appendix A). If the mover participates in a dispute resolution program, you may find submitting your claim to arbitration under such a program a less expensive and more convenient way to seek recovery. Movers who participate in a dispute resolution program are required to advise all customers of the existence and details of the program before they accept a shipment to be transported. If the mover does not provide information about a dispute resolution program at the time an order for service is prepared, you should ask whether the mover participates in such a program.

Points to Remember

- Movers may give binding estimates.
- Nonbinding estimates may not be accurate; actual charges may often exceed the estimate.
- Specify pickup and delivery dates in the order for service.
- The bill of lading is your contract with the mover. Read it carefully. If you have any questions, ask your mover or call the ICC.
- Be sure that you understand the extent of your mover's liability for loss and damage.
- You have the right to be present each time your shipment is weighed.
- You may request a reweigh of your shipment.
- If you have moved on a nonbinding estimate, you should have enough cash or a certified check to pay the estimated cost of your move plus 10 percent more at time of delivery.

If You're Not Satisfied

Losses and damages do occasionally occur when a moving company moves your belongings. What can you do if you cannot come to a mutually agreeable solution with the moving company? The American Movers Conference (AMC), the national trade association that represents carriers and agents in the household-goods moving industry, has established an arbitration program that is a less costly way to settle disputes than a court procedure. In 1996, the U.S. Department of Transportation made it mandatory that moving companies participate in the Dispute Settlement Program for Household Goods Shippers. To maintain impartiality, the program is administered by the American Arbitration Association, an independent, nonprofit organization not affiliated with the AMC, any mover, or the U.S. government.

How to Request Arbitration

Within 60 days of the time a mover makes a final offer or denies a claim, you may write to the American Movers Conference, Dispute Settlement Program, at 1622 Duke Street, Alexandria, VA 22314, requesting arbitration.

In your letter, include the name of the mover, the identification number of your shipment, the dates and location of pickup and delivery, and a description of the loss, including cost. If your dispute meets the arbitration program guidelines, the AMC will notify the mover and send you a description of the program and forms to fill out. If you wish to continue, you must fill out and return the forms along with $150, your half of the cost of instigating arbitration proceedings. The mover also submits information about the dispute and $150. The arbitrator will then examine all the evidence and generally reach a decision within 60 days.

Is Arbitration Legally Binding?

Yes, the arbitrator's decision is legally binding on both parties involved in the dispute. The arbitrator has jurisdiction only covering claims for loss or damage to the household goods transported, or such other disputes arising out of the transportation of household goods that are mutually agreed upon, in writing, by both the consumer and the mover. The arbitrator cannot consider other claims such as loss of wages, punitive damages, or violations of law. Usually, the amount of any award may not exceed the carrier's liability as outlined in the bill of lading. You may obtain more information about the AMC Dispute Settlement Program for Household Goods Shippers from your moving company or directly from the AMC.

Figuring the Total Cost of the Move

When figuring what it will cost you to move with the help of a mover, remember there are several costs involved besides just the cost of the moving company. If your new home is more than a few hours away, you will have to compute the cost of travel. This will include your personal transportation costs (gas for your car, airline or other tickets, etc.), food, lodging, and other incidentals. Depending on how you construct your moving budget, you may also want to include the cost of cleaning and repairing the home you are leaving as well as the one you are moving into. You may have costs for transporting animals or unusual items, and day-care costs for young children or the elderly or disabled.

How *Your Mover Can Help*

Before you choose a mover to transport all your goods from your old home to your new home, you should speak with representatives of several different moving companies. Each one of them will be able to offer you help and answer your many questions. Each company will have a packet of information to give you. Accept all those packets and go through them later. You will find lots of helpful tips, from questions to ask potential movers, to how to pack Aunt Hattie's antiques, to what to pack versus what to carry with you in the car. There will also be reminders of whom to notify of your move and suggestions on how to move plants and pets.

Once you decide on a mover, you will have a representative of the company to call on for advice and information. That person will explain exactly what services are provided, what tasks you will be expected to perform yourself, how your houseful of belongings will be handled, what you can anticipate on moving day, and when your things will be delivered to your new home.

Commonly Asked Questions

Q. Why should I hire a mover?

A. Obviously, hiring a mover makes the task much easier for you and your entire family. It's easy to make the decision if your employer is footing the bill. But there are many other times when it makes sense to hire the job out. If your budget allows, by all means let the professionals ensure that your belongings arrive at your new home in top condition. They have the knowledge, experience, equipment, and materials to accomplish the job in the least time, with the least mess, and the least damage, loss, or breakage. Also, your family routine will be interrupted less if you can have a moving company come in with a crew to pack and load efficiently and quickly. If you do not have the good health and strength to pack, lift, carry, and load as many as 150 or more boxes as well as all your furniture and appliances, a mover may be your best choice. So, while you might undertake a do-it-yourself move across town, give serious consideration to letting the professionals help if you are moving across the country.

Q. If I hire a mover, how can I save money?

A. You can still save a substantial amount of money by doing some of the work yourself. For example, you can pack some or all of your household goods yourself, then let the movers load it all onto the truck. When you interview moving companies, ask about all their services, and which ones you can perform yourself to save money.

Q. Why is a full inventory of my goods important?

A. Without a full inventory of your goods, it could take months, or even years, before you realize something was lost along the way. Also, if you note the condition of items on your inventory, you have a record in case something is damaged in transit.

Q. Is my shipment insured by the mover?

A. Unless you make specific arrangements, the mover assumes liability for your entire shipment at an amount equal to $1.25 per pound times the weight of your shipment. Be sure to discuss insurance with your mover and secure adequate coverage for the value of your belongings.

CHAPTER 6

Moving on a Budget

Moving on a budget usually means doing all or almost all of the work yourself. According to one truck rental company, three-quarters of all movers are do-it-yourselfers. That means that of the 40 to 50 million people who will move sometime during the next near, as many as 37 million of them will do the work themselves, using all or mostly volunteer help and their own, borrowed, or rented equipment, including the moving vehicle. On average, a do-it-yourself move can save one-third to one-half the cost of a moving company move. But it takes a big commitment from each member of the family.

This chapter looks at many of the aspects of moving yourself. Are you and your family do-it-yourselfers?

Borrowing a Truck or Trailer

If you are moving a short distance, across town, or to a neighboring town, you may be able to accomplish it all in a few small truck or trailer loads, depending on how many possessions you have. If you don't own a truck or trailer, a good friend may loan you one for a day or two. Be sure to return it cleaned out, washed, and with a full tank of gas. If the loaner won't allow you to pay a few bucks for the use of the vehicle, take him or her out to dinner or otherwise show your thanks.

Don't borrow a vehicle that isn't in good running condition. Think how frustrating it would be to be stuck at the side of the road for several hours while your unloading crew waits at the new house!

When you borrow *any* vehicle, check on insurance coverage for the vehicle, yourself, and the goods you are moving. If your auto or household insurance does not cover it automatically, you may be able to purchase short-term special coverage. Get all these questions answered before the day of the move.

Renting a Truck or Trailer

Make reservations early if you need to rent a truck or trailer, especially in the summer when truck rental companies are busiest. If you make your reservations at least a month before your move, you are more likely to get exactly the truck or trailer you want. If you rent from a national truck rental company, they must schedule the vehicle you want because their fleet travels the entire country. When you rent from a national firm, you can pick up the truck in your current hometown and return it to the nearest dealer in your new hometown when you are finished. If your move is local, you can also check out small, local rental companies.

If possible, schedule your move between Sunday and Thursday, when fewer demands are made on rental equipment and fewer people are on the road. Weekends at the end of the month are the absolute busiest.

How will you choose a truck rental company? If you live in a small town, you may have to use whoever is available or travel a ways to pick up and drop off your unit. If you live in a city, be a savvy consumer. Call several companies and ask lots of questions. How many trucks/trailers do they have? How old are the vehicles? Automatic or manual transmission? Gas or diesel engine? How many miles to the gallon can you expect when the truck is full? What happens if the truck breaks down? Does the truck have a ramp or hydraulic lift? Is the cab air-conditioned? How many adults can ride comfortably? What packing and loading materials do they provide or sell? After you have narrowed down the field, go look at the equipment. If you are moving across the country, you will be spending several days in the cab of that truck. It will be worth a few dollars more to have a clean, comfortable ride. You don't want to be in the middle of the desert in August without air-conditioning.

Most rental companies will need the following information to make your reservation: your name and telephone number, a major credit card number, the date of your move, your current town, your destination, and the size of truck or trailer you will need.

☞ **Money-$aving Tip #24** *Make reservations for your truck or trailer rental early. It can be costly to have to drive to the neighboring town, or even further, to rent a truck.*

Determining Your Moving Vehicle Needs

Your family's moving needs are different from your neighbor's. You may need a 26-foot van to hold your furniture, appliances, tools, and toys, while your neighbor may be able to move in a small, enclosed trailer.

This section will help you determine the best vehicle for your move.

If You Need a Truck

The following guidelines from truck rental companies, based on years of experience, will help you decide which truck to rent. These are only starting guidelines and must be adjusted if you believe your home holds more or less than average. Even if your move is just across town, it may be more efficient to rent a truck that will hold everything in one trip. When you compare costs, be sure to consider fuel and remember that your time is valuable. It is more exhausting to make several trips than to pack up one truck and get it all there at once. Making several trips rather than one or two could even mean that you end up paying for a second day's rental on the truck.

You may be able to move out of a condominium or apartment with a small truck, up to about 10 feet. It should hold the furniture from a small dwelling, plus about 15 boxes of personal items.

The contents of a one- or two-bedroom home of up to about 1,200 square feet can usually be loaded onto a 14- or 15-foot truck, with room for furniture, appliances, and about 35 boxes.

If you are moving out of a two- or three-bedroom home of up to 1,600 square feet, you will probably require a 17- or 18-foot truck, allowing for about 50 boxes in addition to large items.

A three- or four-bedroom home of up to 2,000 square feet will require a truck of about 24 feet to hold furniture, appliances, yard and garage items, and about 70 boxes.

If the home you are leaving is a four-bedroom home of more than 2,000 square feet, you will want to rent a truck of at least 26 feet to hold everything, including as many as 120 boxes of personal and household items.

☞ **Money-$aving Tip #25** *Rent a truck or trailer that will hold your possessions without much extra space. Unless your move is very short, it is usually more economical to make your move in one trip, rather than use a smaller vehicle and make several trips.*

If You Need a Trailer

In some moves, you might be able to get it all transported in a trailer. If you are moving away from your parents' home for the first time, if you are moving into a furnished retirement home, or if you are one of those people who always travels light, you may be able to move all your possessions in a trailer as small as 4×6 feet. A covered trailer will protect your belongings far better than an open trailer.

If you are moving out of a two-room residence, you should be able to get everything into a 5×8-foot trailer, including about 20 boxes. Possessions from a three-room home, including approximately 35 boxes, should fit into a 6×12-foot trailer.

When you consider using a trailer to make a move, you must consider the type and condition of your tow vehicle. Check the radiator. Even though it has not given you any previous trouble, your car may overheat when pulling a loaded trailer over a mountain pass. Check your brakes. They will have to stop a heavier load than ever before. Be sure the car is tuned up and in top condition. Everything you save by moving yourself with a borrowed or rented trailer can quickly be eaten up with the expense of a breakdown.

Trailer Hitches

A hitch is required to pull a trailer. If your car is not equipped with a hitch, you will need to either rent (if you can find anyone to rent you one) or purchase and install one on your car. Check your owner's manual to determine the largest size trailer your car can safely tow. Install only a hitch that meets your car's specifications. Some truck rental companies will sell and install hitches, but you can also do it yourself or have it done elsewhere. Check around for price and quality.

Towing Your Car

If you move in a borrowed or rented truck, you may wish to tow your car to your new home. The easiest way is with a specially designed car carrier, available from truck rental companies. It's easy to load and unload your car and there is no wear on tires or any other part of your car. You can also rent tow bars and tow dollies. For extra storage, you can place a cartop carrier on your car. Just be careful not to exceed the weight limit of the trailer or hitch.

How Much Help Do You Need?

How much help is enough and when does it get to be too much? It's an overwhelming job to try to move everything yourself, even with a dolly and a good ramp to your truck. One helper will lighten the load considerably. Three or four good, strong workers will make short work of the loading and unloading. Another crew of three or four to pack final boxes and prepare everything for the loaders is helpful. And a third crew for cleanup would be ideal. If you have appliances to move, give yourself and your helpers a break and rent an appliance dolly. A utility dolly will help in moving boxes and many other items. These dollies can be rented from your truck rental company.

Once again, remember to reward your help with cold (nonalcoholic) drinks and sandwiches or other refreshments. Moving is hard, thirsty work.

Insurance

As mentioned earlier, be sure to check into insurance coverage whenever your rent or borrow another vehicle. Check with your homeowner's and your auto insurance company to determine comprehensive and collision coverage of the vehicle and coverage of the contents you are moving. If you rent a truck or trailer, be sure you understand the extent of the coverage the rental company offers and compare it with an extra coverage you may be able to purchase from your regular insurance company.

Neglecting to obtain adequate insurance coverage can be a costly oversight.

Driving a Truck

It's not for everyone, and it may not be for you. Critically and impartially assess your driving skills and experience before you get behind the wheel of a truck. Your life, your passengers' lives, and the lives of others on the road depend on your ability as a driver.

If you do decide to borrow or rent a truck and drive it yourself, talk to the owner and/or read any literature from the rental company. Ask if there are any special quirks you should know about. One family learned the hard way that the parking brakes on the truck they borrowed held only if a foot was on the brake pedal when the parking brake was applied. Take a test drive. Practice backing up. Learn to use the side mirrors. Ask a professional truck driver's advice. Following are just a few tips for making the drive more safe:

- Use your seat belt and require that any passengers use theirs.
- Never drink and drive.

- Set the side mirrors before you pull out and use them often.
- Start out slowly and get the feel of the truck.
- Watch your mirrors during turns to learn how much extra space you need.
- Allow extra time when merging into traffic because it takes longer for a truck to accelerate than it does for a car.
- Allow extra time and distance for stopping because it also takes longer to stop a truck than it does a car.
- Observe special truck speed limits as posted on highways. Expect that your trip will take longer than it would in a car.
- Don't be in a hurry. If you must pass, allow plenty of time and space.
- If you are not used to driving a truck, avoid backing up if possible.
- If you must back up, let your assistant spot you as you back into the driveway or other location.
- Know what your overhead clearance is and watch for low bridges or tunnels, service station canopies, motel entrances, drive-up windows, and other obstacles.

Pulling a Trailer

As with driving a truck, before you tow a trailer of any kind, evaluate your driving experience and knowledge of towing. If you do decide to tow a trailer, again ask for and read any advice from an experienced driver or your rental company. The following tips will also help:

- Use your seat belt and require that passengers use theirs.
- Set your mirrors and use them often.
- Test your brakes. It will take longer to stop with the added weight.
- Check your auto manual or ask at your tire store. Your tires may need extra inflation to carry the load

- Watch your radiator indicator. Your car could overheat with the extra weight to pull.
- Check the hitch each time you stop to be sure safety chains and latches are secure.
- Avoid backing up if possible. Think ahead and plan your stops so you don't have to back out, even if it means walking further.
- If you must back up, place your hands on the bottom of the wheel at approximately four and eight instead of two and ten, gripping the wheel from the inside, and go slowly.
- Rely on a spotter to back up. Agree on signals. Spotter, remember that if you can't see the driver in the mirror, the driver can't see you.

Pulling a Trailer with a Truck

If you need to move your car or another object, such as a boat, or if your possessions require a truckload, plus a trailer, your driving task will be more difficult, especially if you are not an experienced truck driver. When deciding how to get everything from here to there, calculate the total length of the combination you may be piloting down the freeway. It may be intimidating! If you do need to take such a combination, allow extra time for your trip and consider the following tips:

- As always, use seat belts.
- Set your mirrors and use them often.
- Remember, the more weight, the longer it will take to stop your rolling vehicle.
- Plan ahead. It may not be easy to find a place to park a 40-plus-foot rig.
- Backing up can be even more tricky. It's not a good alternative, but if you cannot see the sides of the vehicle being towed, you can attach a horizontal flag that will extend to where you can see it in your side mirror.

- Follow the backing-up procedure described in the section above.
- If you get into a tight spot and cannot seem to maneuver out of it, relax, admit the problem, and try to find an experienced truck driver to lend a hand.

Storing Your Goods

If your new home is not ready when you have to move out of your old home, or if your new home is significantly smaller than your old one, you may need to rent a storage unit. Some large truck rental companies offer at least short-term storage. Ask them for prices and compare with other store-it-yourself options for the best price. At least one national truck rental company currently offers short-term storage free with one-way truck rental. When researching storage options, ask about insurance coverage while your belongings are in storage.

Calculating the Cost of a Do-It-Yourself Move

There are a number of cost factors even in a do-it-yourself move. The list below will help you come up with a total cost for moving:

- Truck or trailer rental
- Tow bar or car carrier rental
- Drop-off charges (if applicable)
- Other equipment rental (dollies, furniture pads)
- Packing materials (boxes, tape, etc.)
- Any labor you employ to help pack or load
- Insurance
- Fuel
- Mileage
- Motels
- Meals
- Storage

Chapter 8 will help you determine the amount or packing materials and furniture pads you will need. Also, remember when you are calculating the cost of moving yourself, unless you are experienced and knowledgeable about packing and loading a truck, there may be more damage to your belongings than if they were packed and loaded by a professional.

☞ **Money-$aving Tip #26** *When you are figuring costs, be sure to include the cost of fuel for your rental truck. Ask the rental agent about the truck's miles per gallon when it is loaded. Just to be safe, increase the figure a bit more when you make your calculations.*

Loading a Truck or Trailer for Safe Transport

Proper loading of your truck or trailer will make the drive easier and safer. A loosely packed load can shift and cause the truck and trailer or towing vehicle to sway, which can even lead to loss of control. A poorly balanced load can make driving harder and even cause damage to the towing vehicle. And a poorly packed truck or trailer can lead to damage of your furniture and other possessions. It's well worth the time to plan how your truck or trailer should be loaded, and to follow your plan. While you are taking your time loading, remember that unloading will be much quicker.

First of all, whether loading a trailer or a truck, wrap all of your furniture and appliances in moving pads. It may seem expensive to rent so many of them, but otherwise you take a chance on having things arrive at your new home with new scratches or gouges. You can also use old blankets, pillows, sleeping bags, and similar items as furniture wraps.

Next, mentally divide your truck or trailer into quarters. You will load it a quarter at a time, working from floor to ceiling and packing it as solidly as possible. Think square.

FIGURE 6.1 Load large, heavy items in front. Stack lighter boxes on top of heavier boxes. Pack tightly.

Try to create heavy squares as the first level of your load, and build up from there. For example, you can fit two, three, or four pieces together to make a rectangle or square, then wrap them all together with a furniture wrap. Once a quarter of the space is packed, tie it off with rope. Fill any small spaces with boxes or other small items.

The key to efficient loading is to pack tightly. Use all available space. Put boxes under chair legs. Place long, flat pieces under sofas and other furniture with legs. Leave lightweight items in furniture drawers. You get the idea. Now, let's get more specific.

Loading a Truck

Moving trucks have different features, but most of the guidelines below apply to most trucks (see Figure 6.1):

- Back the truck as close as possible to the door of your home. If possible, extend the loading ramp to the top step of your house.

- Pack fragile items, such as electronics, in the overhead space over the cab.
- Load large, heavy items first. Put the refrigerator at the front, across from the washer and dryer for good weight distribution.
- Load other heavy items toward the front of the truck.
- Place mattresses, box springs, tabletops, and other long, flat items along the sides of the truck. A large mirror will travel safely between a mattress and box spring. Tie down whatever goes along the walls.
- Put heavy boxes on the bottom. Boxes of about the same size, strength, and weight can be stacked. Put lighter boxes on top of heavy ones, but don't put heavy boxes on top of light ones.
- Load dressers and desks so that their drawers face the wall, keeping them from opening.
- Place lightweight or oddly shaped items on top of the load.
- Load a box of items you will need at the new house where it will come off the truck first. Include items such as toilet tissue and other necessities.
- Lock the truck when it is all loaded.

Loading a Trailer

Loading a trailer is not really much different from loading a truck. Professionals suggest that you place at least 60 percent of the weight of the load in the front half of the trailer. The weight should be evenly distributed from side to side to prevent swaying of the trailer (see Figure 6.2).

Otherwise, follow the guidelines above for loading a truck.

FIGURE 6.2 Properly distributing the weight of the load will make towing a trailer easier.

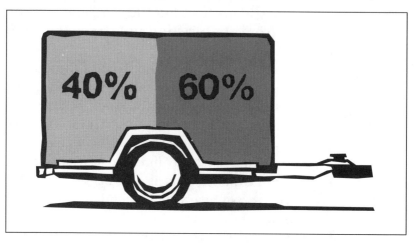

How Your Mover Can Help

A good truck rental firm will offer you lots of advice and assistance in your move. They will help you determine the size of truck or trailer you need, and advise you on how much packing material you need to purchase. They will sell you the packing materials, from tape to wardrobe boxes. They will suggest how many furniture pads you should rent, and may even advise you on the best route to your destination.

They can tell you how much mileage you can expect from the truck (be sure to ask for *loaded* mileage, because an empty truck takes far less fuel). They will furnish brochures that will graphically instruct you on the best and safest way to load your truck or trailer. They will tell you what to do if you have a breakdown in their vehicle. Be sure to carry their toll-free number with you on moving day.

Commonly Asked Questions

Q. How do I know what size truck to rent?

A. Your rental dealer can help, but basically the following guidelines should help: apartment/condo, 10-foot truck; one- to two-bedroom home, 14- or 15-foot truck; two- to three-bedroom home, 17- or 18-foot truck; three- to four-bedroom home, 24-foot truck; and a larger home, 26-foot truck or more.

Q. I've never driven a truck. Can I do it?

A. You must judge yourself as a truck driver. If you are borrowing the truck, ask to drive it around a few blocks before moving day to see how it handles and if you feel comfortable driving it. If you rent a truck, be sure it is a late model with all the conveniences to make it easier to handle: power steering, good brakes, automatic transmission, good mirrors, and air-conditioning for comfort if you must travel in the heat of the summer.

Q. What about pulling a trailer?

A. With the right equipment, most drivers can pull at least a small trailer. Again, judge your driving ability and experience before making a commitment. Don't attempt to pull a trailer larger or heavier than the owner's manual for your car recommends. Use an adequate mirror system.

Q. If I'm driving a truck, how can I get my car to my new home?

A. Sometimes it's easiest to have another driver take the car. Otherwise, you can rent a car carrier, tow dolly, or tow bar, whichever you and your rental agent agree is the best choice for your situation. The added weight will take a toll on your fuel mileage and make your drive slower.

Q. What are the basics of loading a truck or trailer?

A. Load heavier items toward the front of the truck or trailer. Balance the load from side to side. Pack tightly. Place mattresses and other similar items along the walls and tie them down. Stack boxes heaviest to lightest. Place oddly shaped and lightweight items on top.

CHAPTER 7

Organizing a Stress-Free Move

Organization is the most important element of a stress-free move. An organized move will be much easier on the entire family, and it will save money. It's never too early to start planning your move. The more lead time you have, the easier and less stressful your transition will be.

If you have only a short time in which to prepare for your move, planning is even more important. Spending an hour or so planning your move on paper can save you hours of stress and wondering if everything is getting done.

☞ **Money-$aving Tip #27** *Organize your move. By planning things out and knowing what to expect, you can see many ways to save money. For example, if you wait until the last minute to make arrangements with a moving company, you may end up using the most costly service. If you plan ahead, you will have time to get estimates and be able to choose the most economical, yet reliable, mover.*

Start now to make it easier on yourself.

Eight Things You Can Do Now to Reduce Stress

1. Begin Decluttering

If you are lucky enough to know about your move months in advance, you can easily and slowly examine all your belongings and determine which are really valuable enough to move. If you have just a short time to prepare, getting rid of at least some of the big extras will simplify your job. Set up your own criteria for what to save, what to send to the dump, what to sell, and what to give away. If you haven't used it or worn it in the past year, will you use or wear it again? If it needs repair, will it be fixed or should it be replaced after the move?

Enlist the entire family. Almost everyone should be able to go through their belongings and find lots of items to dispose of. Small children may need help. Give everyone containers to fill. You may have to be the one to determine what is bound for the dump and what might sell at your moving sale. Start with the attic and the basement. Go through every drawer and every closet in every room. Evaluate each piece of furniture and appliance. Is it time to sell or give away the stroller, high chair, crib, swing, and car seat? Babies add a lot of furniture! Have you ever used the hot dog cooker Aunt Julie sent you as a wedding gift?

As soon as you decide to move, begin sorting and eliminating. Families with grown children often need to add another step, notifying the young adults that they must remove their belongings from the old family home. Give them a deadline! If it isn't gone by that deadline, you have the right to dispose of it as you see fit.

Moving just might provide a welcome opportunity to replace some of that old furniture and replenish your wardrobe. Besides, it feels good to declutter and simplify.

☞ **Money-$aving Tip #28** *Declutter your home. Don't move anything you no longer use or can replace more economically than you can move it. Moving companies charge by the weight of the shipment; the less you ship, the lower the cost. And if you are moving yourself, you will need a smaller truck if you eliminate unneeded goods, which means a lower rental fee and less fuel consumption.*

2. Plan to Escape the Chaos Regularly

Especially as the moving date draws near, you can reduce stress by regularly taking a break from the confusion and activity. Take an hour a day for yourself. Use it to exercise, go out for lunch, read a good book, relax with your spouse, or whatever helps you through the day. Also plan at least one morning, afternoon, or evening of leisure activity per week. Play golf, go to dinner and a movie, indulge in a picnic, go horseback riding; do something just for fun. Taking a break from the extra stress of preparing for a move in addition to all your regular activities will be a lifesaver.

3. Plan a Moving Calendar

Sketch out a rough moving calendar. Use a wall or desk calendar or make your own. The important thing is to get a visual image of the moving tasks that need to be completed and an idea of when. As your move edges closer, you can fill in more details and begin to cross off completed tasks. It may be easiest to start with moving day and plan backward, allowing ample time to complete each task.

No task is too small to list. Your calendar should include everything from "Decide on a moving company" to "Notify milkman to stop delivery" to "Return library books." Get the whole family involved in creating the calendar and in completing tasks that can be crossed off the calendar. Once something is written down on the calendar you can forget worrying about it and know that it will be remembered and done at the proper time. Just remember to refer to your calendar often!

4. Start a Moving Notebook

Buy a small notebook to carry with you. In it you can make all kinds of notes about your move as they occur to you. You will be a master of list-making before you are settled in your new home. Many of the notes will transfer to your calendar when you have a chance. The notebook can also be used as a daily reminder of errands that need to be handled. It can contain lists of people to contact for stopping services at your old house and starting them at the new house; addresses of people to notify of your move; and lists of resources about your new hometown, state, or neighborhood. It will become an invaluable companion.

5. Prepare and Freeze Meals for the Most Hectic Days

If your move is within a month or two, now would be a good time to prepare and freeze several meals to serve during the last couple weeks before moving when there will be days no one has time to cook and a fast-food hamburger just won't satisfy your hunger. Casseroles and other one-dish meals are perfect. You can just add a fresh salad (the packaged green salads are handy and easy), bread, and fresh fruit for dessert, and you will be amazed at the return of energy.

6. Begin Gathering Information about Moving, Movers, and Destinations

If you know where you are moving, now is a good time to contact the local chamber of commerce and other sources of information about your new hometown. Even if you haven't had a chance to visit your new home, reading about it and seeing photos of it can help make it feel more familiar. Depending on your moving budget, you can also call moving companies and rental truck companies to gather information on moving services and costs.

7. Hold a Family Meeting to Discuss the Move and Responsibilities

Once the whole family knows about the move, hold a family conference to talk about everyone's feelings, to share all the information you have about the move and your destination, and to divide moving responsibilities. Each family member, from toddler to grandparent, has completely unique feelings about the move. Those feelings may include apprehension, excitement, resentment, confusion, and many other emotions. Encourage everyone to share their feelings. Listen to each family member and help alleviate negative feelings.

Share any information you have about the move and your destination. Let everyone know what they will be able to move. If the move is just across town, your decluttering will probably be less stringent than if the move is 2,500 miles away. And if the move is temporary, especially out of the country, some items may be put in storage. If you have a new home picked out, try to have photos of it, even a video if possible, so that each family member can begin to mentally move into the new house. Talk about who will get which bedroom and how the family room will be used. Discuss the use of the extra room over the garage with your teenagers. Share any information you have about the new city, state, or region of the country. If Johnny has always wanted to ski, let him know that there is a ski area just two hours from your new home. If you're moving to Southern California or Florida, make a ceremony of getting rid of the snow shovel. Talk about what you will do in the new home and town.

Divide up moving responsibilities among those who can reasonably be expected to help with the move. Each individual can sort his or her own belongings, and if you are doing part or all of the move yourselves, each one can pack his or her own items. Someone needs to be in charge of notifying others of your move; someone needs to plan and orchestrate the overall move (coordinating with the mover, etc.); someone needs to find new doctors, schools, and other resources in the new town. There are plenty of jobs to keep everyone busy and productive. Plan to have family meetings throughout the moving process, including several after the move to help any family member who might be having extra trouble adjusting to the new environment.

☞ **Money-$aving Tip #29** *Unless the swing set or other awkward yard toys are brand new, think about treating the kids to something new at the new house. Such items take up a lot of space in a rental truck or moving van.*

8. Find a Good Real Estate Agent

A good real estate agent will help you sell your home for the best price and help you purchase your dream home. Even if your destination is out of your current area, a good agent will have contacts all across the country to help you locate your next home. A good agent can often give you at least preliminary information about your new neighborhood, city, or state.

☞ **Money-$aving Tip #30** *If you have the information, sketch a floor plan and decide upon furniture placement. If something won't fit, don't go to the expense of moving it.*

Your Moving Schedule

You may be surprised at how much you can do regarding your move well ahead of time. Anything you can finish and cross off your moving calendar a month or even two before the move, the less stress you will feel during those last few weeks and days before moving day.

Get out your moving calendar and start it with notations of the following tasks.

Two Months Before Moving Day

❑ Get estimates from at least four moving companies if you will use a mover.
❑ Get costs from at least two truck rental companies if you will move yourself.
❑ Sketch out a floor plan of your new home for furniture and appliance placement.
❑ Make an inventory of your household goods and begin to declutter (start with the basement, attic, garage, and other storage areas).
❑ Start a file for all your moving paperwork (estimates, receipts, etc.).
❑ Arrange to transfer school records.
❑ Choose a mover (or truck rental company).

Six Weeks Before Moving Day

❑ Obtain and fill out post office change-of-address cards.
❑ Subscribe to the paper in your new hometown.
❑ Make arrangements for storage if necessary.
❑ Ask doctors, etc., for referrals and obtain all medical records.
❑ Have antiques, pieces of art, and other valuables appraised.
❑ Clean all closets and drawers.

❑ Start using foods and cleaning supplies that cannot be moved.

Four Weeks Before Moving Day

❑ Contact all utilities for service disconnection at your old home and connection at your new home. Be sure disconnect is the day *after* you leave and connection the day *before* you arrive.
❑ If you are moving yourself, reserve a rental truck.
❑ If you are packing yourself, obtain packing materials and start packing items you won't need until after you arrive at the new house.
❑ Arrange for cleaning and repair of furniture, drapes, and carpeting.
❑ Arrange for special transportation of your pets and plants if necessary.
❑ Check with your insurance company to see how your possessions are covered during transit.
❑ Make any travel plans necessary for your move.
❑ Check to see if you need any moving permits.
❑ Plan your moving sale.

Three Weeks Before Moving Day

❑ Dispose of items that cannot be moved, such as inflammable liquids.
❑ Prepare auto registration for transfer (if moving to another state).
❑ If you are moving in or out of an apartment, arrange for use of the elevator.
❑ Make child-care arrangements for moving day.
❑ Hold your moving sale.

Two Weeks Before Moving Day

❏ Arrange for disposal of anything not sold at your moving sale.
❏ Service your car in preparation for the move.
❏ Return any borrowed items (including library books) and retrieve any loaned items.
❏ Cancel newspaper delivery.
❏ Notify any creditors of your move.
❏ Transfer prescriptions and be sure you have an adequate supply of medications on hand.
❏ Assemble a file folder of information to leave for the new owner of your home.

One Week Before Moving Day

❏ Transfer your bank accounts.
❏ Take animals to vet for immunizations if necessary.
❏ Close your safe-deposit box.
❏ Settle any bills with local businesses.
❏ Drain power equipment of oil and gas.
❏ Drain water hoses.
❏ Find new homes for plants that will not be moved.
❏ Confirm any travel reservations.

Two to Three Days Before Moving Day

❏ Drain your water bed.
❏ Defrost refrigerator and freezer, propping doors open.
❏ Let movers pack your belongings (unless it's a do-it-yourself move).
❏ Disconnect and prepare major appliances for move.
❏ Set aside anything that will travel in your car so it will not be loaded on the truck.
❏ Pack a box of items that will be needed first at the new house.

❑ Obtain cash or traveler's checks for the trip and to pay the movers.
❑ Confirm arrival time of your moving van.
❑ If moving yourself, dismantle beds and other large furniture.

Moving Day

❑ If using a mover, be sure someone is at the old house to answer questions.
❑ Note all utility meter readings.
❑ Read your bill of lading and inventory carefully before signing. Keep this paperwork in a safe place.

Delivery Day

❑ Again, be on hand to answer any questions.
❑ Check your belongings carefully and note on the inventory any damaged items.
❑ On an interstate move, be prepared to pay the driver before your possessions are unloaded.
❑ Supervise unloading and unpacking.
❑ Be prepared to pay your mover with cash, certified check, or traveler's checks unless other arrangements have been made in advance.

People/Businesses to Notify of Your Move

❑ Employer
❑ Electric company
❑ Gas/Oil company
❑ Local telephone service
❑ Long distance telephone service
❑ Water/Sewer
❑ Trash service
❑ Post office

❏ Magazines
❏ Newspapers
❏ Charge Accounts
❏ Banks/Credit unions/Loan companies
❏ Schools
❏ Doctors/Dentists/Other medical professionals
❏ Attorney/Accountant
❏ Veterinarian
❏ Church
❏ Clubs/Organizations
❏ Department of Motor Vehicles
❏ Relatives/Friends
❏ Tax assessors
❏ Delivery companies, such as diapers and bottled water
❏ Service companies such as cable TV and lawn care

☞ **Money-$aving Tip #31** *Check with ongoing medical care givers, such as the orthodontist or obstetrician, about services for which you have prepaid. You may be able to get a refund or transfer some credit to a new practitioner.*

Organizing and Holding Your Moving Sale

Most of us hesitate to dispose of never-used, seldom-used, worn out, or even broken or ill-fitting items. Moving offers the perfect excuse to pare down, reduce the work and cost of shipment, and even earn a little cash while doing so.

You probably have a good supply of things to sell, everything from clothing to kitchen gadgets, to exercise equipment, to snow shovels and lawn mowers. Remember that anything you do not somehow get rid of has to be packed, loaded, unloaded, unpacked, and placed in your new home. If it's shabby, nearly worn out, ill-fitting, out-of-style, or seldom used, seriously consider parting with it. If you haven't held a sale before or attended others, you may be surprised at how many of your unwanted items will find willing buyers. Your sale will be even more profitable if it is well organized.

Hold your sale as soon as possible. It will simplify your moving schedule. Ask your neighbors and friends if they would like to combine sales. Shoppers like to see lots of goods at once. Saturdays are the best days for a moving or yard sale, but be sure to avoid holiday weekends when many people have other plans. If you can, hold your sale for two or three days, beginning on Thursday or Friday. Establish a rain date if necessary. Set your sale hours early, as early as 7 A.M. to 3 P.M. if you can, because bargain hunters are notorious for starting early. Even with early hours, be prepared for a few early birds.

Be sure to check with local authorities for regulations on personal sales. In some towns you will need a permit; in others the posting of signs is limited.

Publicize your sale. Your local newspaper will have a classified section for such sales. Include the days, hours, and location of the sale. Call it a moving sale to create extra interest. List a few of the major items you have to sell. Some local radio stations have inexpensive or even free call or write-in announcements of personal items for sale. Post signs wherever you can—at church, work, laundromats, grocery stores, and other businesses. Be sure that any signs you post along the street are easily readable. Use large letters and dark ink (see Figure 7.1). Tell your neighbors, relatives, and friends.

FIGURE 7.1 Make sure your signs are easy to read from the road.

Setting Up for Your Sale

The following tips will help make your sale go more smoothly:

- Save or gather plastic and paper bags and a few boxes for shoppers' convenience.
- Decide where you will hold your sale. Yard? Garage? Basement? More people will stop at your sale if items are clearly visible from the street. People will be more

inclined to step inside to view furniture, appliances, and other large items if you have designed your sale a Moving Sale rather than a Garage or Yard Sale.

- Clearly price all items to be sold. Remember that buyers will want to negotiate a lower price than you set. If your sale involves more than one family, color code, initial, or otherwise mark each item so that proper credit is given.
- Group like items together with signs designating categories, such as "infant clothing" or "games."
- Be sure that items not to be sold are clearly separated from sale items. Make sure the cashier knows what is NOT for sale.
- Offer a table of "giveaways."
- Hang clothing for best display.
- Following local ordinances, post signs at major intersections leading customers to your sale.
- Move your cars down the block or otherwise out of the way to allow for ample parking.
- Make sure everyone has a task for the day. Designate a greeter, a cashier, a bagger, and a carryout. Swap jobs during the day to avoid boredom.
- Offer coffee, tea, ice water, or lemonade as appropriate.
- Prepare a cash box with plenty of change.
- If you accept local checks, get identification, including phone number and address. Issue a receipt.
- Have an electrical outlet available to test small appliances, etc.
- Reduce prices as the sale progresses. Slash prices by at least 50 percent the final day of the sale. Add more items to your "giveaway" table. Remember, the goal is to reduce the bulk of items that you need to move.
- Donate to your favorite charity any items that do not sell. Get a receipt for tax purposes.
- Have fun! Involve the whole family and make your sale day a social event in the neighborhood.

Moving People with Special Needs

Moving people with special needs just takes a little more planning and thought. During your family meetings might be a good time to discuss any special circumstances. People with special needs should be allowed to make as many decisions about their move and care as possible.

The Disabled

As with anyone else, planning provides the key to successfully relocating a family member with a disability. Talk early with any social workers, therapists, doctors, or other professionals who are involved in care.

If you are using a professional moving company, let them know early in your discussions of the special needs that must be considered. Moving company personnel are familiar with the needs of the disabled and will be able to help plan a move that requires the least disruption and discomfort.

If your disabled family member requires a wheelchair, let the mover know and share a floor plan of the new home. This can help the movers plan and know where to place furniture without obstructing wheelchair access.

Providing such special needs as wheelchair ramps, bathroom grab bars, wheelchair-level counters, and others is best accomplished before your move. If possible, once your new home is legally yours, contract for any alterations before moving time so that the disabled person can settle in as quickly as everyone else. If special-needs equipment is to be moved from the old home to the new one, your mover can recommend or arrange for a specialist to dismantle and reassemble such equipment on each end of the move.

While learning about your new neighborhood or city, you will want to gather information on local organizations and services for the disabled. Is there day care available if needed? Do all public buildings include wheelchair access? Is there specialized medical care available nearby?

The Elderly

More and more families are expanding to include multi-generational members. When you or your spouse are transferred or decide to move to another city or state, you might need or want to take Mom or Dad, or both, with you. The U.S. Bureau of the Census predicts that between now and the year 2030, the number of U.S. citizens over 65 will increase by 109 percent, from 33.6 million to 70.2 million people. Today's average life expectancy is near 80 for men and the mid-80s for women. This growing segment of the population often requires assistance with normal daily activities such as meal preparation, home maintenance, and financial care. In the vast majority of cases, that assistance is provided by family members, often including the elderly relative living in the caretaker's home.

With a little extra planning and organizing, an elderly family member can also be moved with as little fuss and disruption as possible. Many of the same questions need to be answered as for a move with a disabled family member. Is there a Senior Citizen Center nearby? Is transportation available? Medical specialists?

If You Are Moving to Another Country

If your moving adventure will take you to foreign shores, your planning will be even more critical and exacting and will include several extra steps. To move to most other countries, you will need to have a passport and a visa. You may also need a work permit and several immunizations, depending on your destination. Make copies of all your vital papers, such as your passport and visa, and carry one extra set with you *separate from the originals* and leave another set in safekeeping with a trusted friend or relative here in the United States. This procedure can save weeks or even months in the event of lost paperwork.

Check with the U.S. State Department for requirements for entry into specific countries. There will be regulations governing what you can and cannot take with you. Check early on regulations concerning pets you wish to move with you. You will also want to know what you can bring back to the United States with you if your move is not permanent.

Finding information on your destination is even more critical when it is outside this country. You will want to learn about the culture, people, laws, education, work conditions, and language of your destination country. If possible, take a course or teach yourself at home at least basic phrases in the native language.

Here are a few other things you can do to prepare for your international move:

- Register your cameras, jewelry, and similar personal items with U.S. Customs so there will be no question upon your reentry.
- Carry a detailed shipping inventory with you and leave a copy at home.
- Be sure you have extra prescriptions and adequate supplies of medications.
- Take an extra pair of prescription glasses with you.
- Obtain an international driver's license.
- Make or update your will.
- Leave a Power of Attorney with a trusted individual.
- Arrange for electric adaptation.

A Few More Planning Tips

Experienced movers know that organization is *the* key to a stress-free move, whether it is just across town or across an ocean. Here are a few more of their suggestions:

- Move on a weekday if you can, when most services are open. Avoid holidays.

- Get address labels with your new address for easy change-of-address notification.
- Designate a packing room and begin early boxing up of items you will not need until after your move. Be sure to label all boxes clearly.
- Plan to use wardrobe boxes so your clothing will arrive clean, still ironed, and ready to wear.
- Pack a box of "arrival essentials" filled with a change of clothes for each family member, toilet paper, sheets, towels, personal toiletries, coffee and coffeemaker, snacks, and whatever else you consider essential for the first few hours in the new house. Make sure this box is loaded either in the car or the truck so that it is unloaded first.

The time and effort you put into planning and organizing your move, the greater the rewards will be. A well-organized move, whether you are moving solo, or moving with three kids, Grandma, two dogs, 16 tropical fish, and a parakeet, can be an adventure of a lifetime, or at least a pleasant experience, while a disorganized move can cause personal stress and enormous friction within a family.

How Your Agent Can Help

Your real estate agent will be a key player in facilitating your stress-free move. Rely on your agent to take some of the hassle out of moving. As soon as you know you will need to move, select an experienced agent whom you feel comfortable with. Let your agent know what your needs and expectations are.

How Your Mover Can Help

Whether you hire a mover or rent a truck and pack, load, unload, and unpack it all yourself, you can get lots of help with your planning. Each mover and rental truck company that you ask for an estimate will probably give you a package of materials concerning moving, including many tips for planning, packing, loading, and settling into your new home. Keep this information for help in planning your move. Some movers include a blank moving calendar that you can fill in with essential tasks. Others even offer free or low-cost videos outlining their services and offering suggestions for making moving easier.

Most moving companies will send representatives to your home to estimate the total weight of your possessions, explain their services, and answer all your questions. Be sure to get a full description of all services because they differ widely among movers. Some offer basic packing and transportation. Others offer more, including relocation services.

Commonly Asked Questions

Q. Why not move everything and sort it all out later?

A. No matter whether you move it all yourself or have a mover do it all, the more you move, the more it will cost. If your employer pays for the move, it is considerate of you to keep costs low. Also, there will be plenty of work and confusion at the new house without having to sort through all possessions and try to get rid of extras there. Besides, it's a very good excuse to weed out what's unnecessary and maybe even replace some of it with new items at the new house.

Q. What is a moving calendar and how would I use it?

A. A moving calendar is a visual schedule of your upcoming move. You can make one on any calendar that has a lot of space to write by each date, or you can make your own. On this calendar you will list all of the tasks associated with moving. Then you can concentrate on accomplishing the tasks rather than worrying about forgetting something that needs to be done.

Q. Should I hold out for top dollar on my moving sale items?

A. Remember, the main goal of the moving sale is to reduce the amount of goods that you have to pack and transport to your new home. Therefore, holding out for top dollar probably is not wise. Better to get a little less and not have to move the item than to hold out for a better price and later have to either give away or move the item.

Q. What will I do with what I don't sell at my moving sale?

A. Get rid of it! Call the Salvation Army, Goodwill, or other reputable charity and let them pick it all up. Get a receipt for tax time. If you really feel you have items of value left, you can call a secondhand dealer to get an estimate.

Q. Isn't it awfully hard to move a disabled or elderly family member?

A. Not really. It may take a little extra planning, but it's certainly no deterrent to moving. Check accommodations along the way and the plan of the new house for accessibility difficulties. Let your mover know early of any special needs. Check with social services and local organizations in your new town for assistance and information.

CHAPTER 8

Packing Techniques and Tips

The most time-consuming chore of your moving project, if you are doing the packing yourself, is the packing of all your personal and household items. You will probably have somewhere between 15 and 150 boxes by the time you finish. You will pack boxes of books, dishes, bathroom articles, hobby items, and mixed boxes of last-minute items that didn't seem to fit in any other categories or boxes.

While one or two adults may need to do the majority of the packing, all members of the family except the very smallest can be in charge of packing their own personal belongings. Share the following rules for packing with everyone who will be packing even one box.

Five Rules for Perfect Packing

The seemingly overwhelming task of packing everything in the house can be simplified and streamlined by following the 5 Rules for Perfect Packing.

Packing Rule Number 1: Plan It All on Paper

Are you surprised? From way back in Chapter 1, we've been talking about planning. Planning each stage and task of the moving process really will make it easier. How many boxes will you need? What size boxes? How many special boxes for lamps, dishes, etc.? How much tape? What kind of markers?

If you've moved a few times before, you will have a good idea of the materials required. If not, the chart later in this chapter will help. Your mover or rental company representative can also give you some guidelines.

Packing Rule Number 2: Use the Best Packing Materials

Sure, you can make the rounds of grocery and liquor stores several times and come up with some usable packing boxes, but they will be of varying sizes, shapes, and durability. If you purchase new or used packing boxes from a moving company or truck rental company, you will have uniform boxes. You can also purchase special boxes for special purposes.

For instance, if you pack your hanging clothing carefully in wardrobe boxes, they will arrive at your new home still clean, pressed, and ready to wear. Don't forget to use all the space in the wardrobe by packing other items at the bottom, underneath your hanging clothing. Dish packs will ensure that your best dinnerware will arrive without chipping or breakage.

If you have a computer, stereo, other electronics, or other delicate items, repack them in their original cartons with the original packing material if possible.

☞ **Money-$aving Tip #32** *Careful packing will save money because items that are packed carelessly or loosely are more vulnerable to breakage. Use good packing materials and take the time to pack well.*

Packing Rule Number 3: Start Packing Early

Give yourself lots of time. You can start packing as soon as you know you will be moving. Start by packing seldom-used items from storage areas such as the attic, basement, or garage. Move on to closets, cupboards, and pantries. Next, pack up decorative items, such as collections, figurines, framed photographs, paintings, and other things nonessential for daily living.

If you follow this rule, much of the work of packing will be completed before the hectic couple of weeks before moving day.

Packing Rule Number 4: Mark Each Box

This sounds simple and easy to do and will be for the first several boxes. But as you go on packing, by box 18 or 47, it's really tempting to get lazy with this task. You'll be sorry later if you allow yourself to slack off. You may even be in a frenzy three days after arrival at the new house when you can't remember which box the toaster oven is in and you still haven't unearthed it from the mountain of boxes.

Use a wide-tip, bright-colored pen for marking boxes. If you followed Packing Rule Number 1 and purchased moving boxes, they probably have special places on them for noting what room they go to and what the contents are. Mark each box in the same place on *two* sides with the *same* information. Note what room the box should be unloaded into, whether kitchen, nursery, John's bedroom, or garage, attic, or basement. List the contents such as games; everyday glasses; wineglasses; toaster, waffle iron, and blender; or household tool set. Be as specific as necessary. It's probably not important to list the name of each game in the box. However, if you have several boxes marked simply "small appliances," you may have to open all of them to find that toaster oven.

Packing Rule Number 5: Establish a Staging Area

You will need somewhere to put all of the boxes that are ready to be loaded onto the truck. Designate a seldom-used room or a portion of the garage as the staging area, and stack boxes that are ready to go neatly within that confined space. On moving day, it will be easy to come in with a utility dolly and load stacks of boxes onto the truck.

If it should be necessary to find something that has already been packed, it will be easy to do if everything is in one area and marked with room designation and contents as suggested in Packing Rule Number 4.

Estimating Your Packing Requirements

If you are hiring a mover to pack, load, and drive your goods to your new home, the mover will bring all the necessary materials and pack your things quickly, efficiently, and safely. With the use of the best packing materials, *you* can also pack quickly, efficiently, and safely.

The best packing materials are available through your mover or through a rental truck company. They will offer square cartons in several sizes, as well as many specialty cartons. You can purchase dish packs, wardrobe boxes, mirror packs, tape, and rope, and even a lock for securing your items once they are all loaded into the truck or trailer.

FIGURE 8.1 Estimating Your Packing Requirements

Size of Your Home	Boxes	Supplies
Small apartment	7-8 small boxes	1 roll tape
1-2 rooms	3-4 medium boxes 3-4 large boxes 2 wardrobes	1 roll rope
1-2 bedrooms up to 1,200 square feet	15 small boxes 8-10 medium boxes 6-8 large boxes 4 wardrobes	2 rolls tape 1 roll rope
2-3 bedrooms 1,200-1,600 square feet	20 small boxes 12-15 medium boxes 8-10 large boxes 6 wardrobes	4 rolls tape 2 rolls rope
3-4 bedrooms 1,600-1,800 square feet	30 small boxes 20 medium boxes 12-15 large boxes 8 wardrobes	5 rolls tape 2 rolls rope
4 or more bedrooms 2,000 or more square feet	40 small boxes 30 medium boxes 20 large boxes 10 wardrobes	6 rolls tape 3 rolls rope

How many boxes will you need? Wardrobes? Rolls of tape? Unless the supplier is far from your home, you can always purchase more supplies if you run out. Also, ask if the supplier will buy back any leftover materials—many will. You may even be able to sell most of the boxes back after your move is completed and everything unpacked. Or, if you move often and have the space, you can break down the boxes and store them for the next move. Many families use those sturdy moving boxes many times over as they relocate from state to state or even country to country.

Figure 8.1 is a rough estimate of the packing materials you can anticipate using if your household is average.

FIGURE 8.2 Cushioning and tight packing are the secrets to a well-padded box.

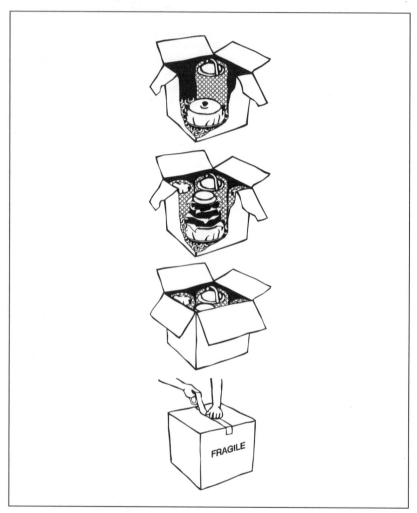

These recommendations are just a starting point. It is quite likely that you will need more boxes than estimated here. You will also need wrapping material, such as bubble wrap, packing peanuts, and/or newspaper. In many cases, you can also use towels, blankets, and other linens as some of your packing material.

How to Pack Everything So It Will Arrive Safely

We're getting down to the real physical work. Taking the time to pack everything carefully to help ensure that it will arrive at the new house in good condition is an investment.

Now that you've purchased your basic supplies, let's get started.

How to Pack a Box

These general instructions will cover the packing of many of your possessions (see Figure 8.2).

1. Put a layer of packing material, such as packing peanuts, in the bottom of the box.
2. Wrap heaviest items in paper or bubble wrap and place in the bottom of the box.
3. Wrap lighter items with paper or bubble wrap. Place them in the box, separated from the heavier items with more packing material.
4. Fill any empty space in the box with peanuts, paper, or other packing material to keep contents from shifting and to keep the box firm.
5. Close and seal the box with strong packing tape. Mark it on two sides for the room it is to go into in the new house and with its contents. You can help your children learn their new address by having them also write the new address on the boxes containing their belongings.

Caution: Do not underpack or overpack boxes. An underpacked box may be crushed in transit, damaging the contents. An overpacked box may burst and the contents may be damaged.

Special Packing Instructions

Here are instructions for carefully packing and transporting your very expensive or bulky possessions.

Antiques—Before packing day, have any valuable antiques appraised by a qualified professional appraiser. Ask your insurance agent, banker, or lawyer to recommend someone. Or you can obtain a copy of the *Directory of Certified Professional Personal Property Appraisers* from the American Society of Appraisers, PO Box 17265, Washington, DC 20041, 800-272-8258. Ask the appraiser if the charge will be a flat rate or by the hour.

If your antiques are truly valuable, you can have a professional packer make specially designed cartons, at extra cost, to hold your pieces. Otherwise, following the rules for safe packing and loading will probably be sufficient. Mark these cartons "fragile."

Small appliances—The carton or box the appliance came in is the best packing material. If it does not include molded packing material or if you do not have the original carton, cushion the appliance with packing peanuts or wadded newspaper.

Bedding—Light items, such as pillows and blankets, can be placed in furniture drawers. Heavier items, such as comforters, should be placed in clean cartons. Bedding can also be used as packing material to cushion other, breakable items. Older bedding can be used as furniture wraps.

Books—Books are heavy. Pack them in small, strong boxes. Place the books cover to cover, alternating bindings. You can pack especially valuable books separately.

☞ **Money-$aving Tip #33** *If you have many books to move, research alternative ways of shipping them, such as book rate through the post office.*

Canned food—Canned food is also heavy. You can reduce the weight and space of your load—and save money—by reducing your food supply before you move. Pack what's left in small, strong cartons. About 25 cans will be enough weight. If necessary, fill the rest of the box with lighter items or packing material. Consider giving away any canned foods left in your cupboards by moving day. Your favorite charity or food pantry will appreciate your generosity.

Clothing—Your hanging clothing will transport best in wardrobe boxes, which hold about 25 garments each. Other items can be packed in the bottom of the wardrobe, under the hanging clothing. Lightweight clothing can be left in dresser and bureau drawers, or it can be packed in suitcases or in clean cartons.

Clocks—Remove the pendulum or secure it to the base of the clock. Wrap and place in a cushioned box. Mark "fragile" on the box.

CD player—Remove all CDs from the player. Draw a diagram of the wiring *before* disconnecting the unit. Remove stacker or multiplay cartridges. If there is a transport screw under the unit, tighten it before packing. Close CD trays.

If you have the original box and packing material, repack the player in it. If not, use a box *slightly larger* than the unit, so that it can be surrounded by packing material. Pack tightly so that the unit will not shift within the box. Mark "fragile" on the box.

Collections—Most collector items should be wrapped separately in clean wrapping paper or bubble wrap and packed into small- to medium-sized cartons, depending on the size and weight. Fill any empty space in the carton with peanuts or other cushioning material. Mark "fragile" on the box.

Computer—First, back up all of your files. Store this backup disk with your original computer disks.

Check your computer manual for the exact procedure for preparing your hard disk and disk drive(s) for moving. You will probably need to be sure the recording heads are parked for transport. IBM and most clones have a SHIP-DISK.EXE program that parks the heads. The hard drive will automatically unpark when you turn it back on.

Turn off the system. Remove all cables from the back of the unit. Mark the cords and wrap them separately. Place the hard drive in its original box with packing material if possible. If not, use sturdy moving boxes and good packing material, such as bubble wrap and/or peanuts. A small blanket may also work well.

The monitor, keyboard, and printer should be treated similarly. If you did not save the original boxes, use sturdy moving boxes and pack securely with bubble wrap and/or packing peanuts. Ink cartridges must be removed from laser printers. Insert a piece of paper in the platen to secure the print head of a pin printer. Mark all of your computer component boxes "fragile."

Curtains/Draperies—Curtains can be folded and placed in drawers or clean cartons. If you are taking your draperies to your new home, have them cleaned, and if your move is within the same town, have them delivered to your new home. Or hang them in wardrobe boxes, still in the cleaning bags.

Dishes—Line a dish pack or a medium-sized carton with crumpled packing paper or newspaper. Wrap each piece separately. Start with a stack of commercial packing paper or newspaper. Place a plate in the center of your packing paper or newspaper. Grasp about two pieces of paper at one corner and pull the paper over the plate. Place a second plate on top of the first one. Take a second corner of the paper and pull over the two stacked plates. Stack a third plate on top of the other two. Grasp the third corner of the paper and pull over the three plates. Repeat with the fourth corner.

Now, turn the stack of wrapped plates over and place in the center of your stack of paper. For extra insurance against breakage, rewrap the bundle. Grasp one corner of the paper and pull over the bundle of plates. Repeat for the second, third, and fourth corners. Seal the bundle with packing tape and place it in a carton with the plates on edge. You can pack all your flatware following this same process.

Put larger items on the bottom and smaller items toward the top of the carton, with cushioning in between layers and over the top layer. You can eliminate dishwashing by first slipping each piece into a clean plastic bag if you are packing with newspaper, or by packing with clean packing paper. Mark "fragile" on the carton.

Glasses and cups—Put crumpled paper inside each glass or cup. Using your own judgment, either wrap each piece separately or nest three or four cups or glasses together. If you nest three or four glasses or cups together, lay them on your stack of paper diagonally. Grasp a corner of the paper and wrap it around the glasses. Repeat with each corner of the paper. Roll into a bundle and secure with tape. Place glasses toward the top of the box, over dishes, etc. Generally, glasses and cups can be packed on their sides, but very fragile items should be packed upright. Mark "fragile" on the carton. (Note: Packing both dishes and glassware is easier with dish packs from a moving company or rental truck company.)

Grandfather clocks—Remove chimes, weights, and pendulums. Use string or wire to secure the weight chains against the base of the close. If yours is a long-distance move, hire an expert to prepare your clock for shipping.

Kitchenware—Nest pots, pans, and similar unbreakable items with paper between pieces. Place heavier items at the bottom of a sturdy carton and lighter items on top.

Lamps—Remove bulbs and wrap separately. Wrap lamp bases in bubble wrap or with towels and place in boxes. Or place them in your freezer or washing machine, with plenty of cushioning material. Wrap lamp shades in clean, white tissue paper or bubble wrap in individual cartons. Mark "fragile" on the carton.

Medicines—Tape the caps of medicine bottles, wrap, and pack upright in a small carton. Be sure to take any you might need along the way in the car with you.

Mirrors/Paintings—For long-distance travel, mirrors and large paintings should be crated for safest handling. Mirror cartons are available through your mover or truck rental agency (see Figure 8.3). Otherwise, these items can be protected in the truck between mattresses or similar items. Smaller mirrors and paintings can be packed in heavy cardboard boxes. Strong tape placed directly across mirrors will help prevent breakage.

Microwave ovens—Remove all loose items from inside the oven. Wrap them and pack in a separate carton. Tape the oven door shut, using an X pattern to keep the door shut and protect the glass as well. Place in the original box with original packing material if you have it. Otherwise, choose a sturdy packing carton slightly larger than the oven and pack tightly with packing material. Mark "fragile" on the box.

Photographs—Your treasured photos will be safest if they are packed in boxes and wrapped between sheets and blankets for extra protection.

FIGURE 8.3 Mirror cartons will protect mirrors and paintings. Other specialty boxes will protect other items.

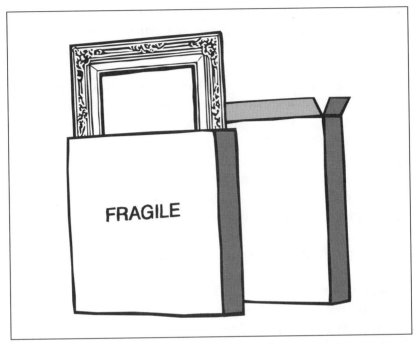

Plants—Most movers will not move your household plants. If they do, it may be expensive. That's just as well because plants probably wouldn't survive a long trip in a moving van. Your climate-controlled car is a better choice for moving plants. If you are moving to another state, be sure to learn whether there are any restrictions on importing plants. The Department of Natural Resources of your new state can provide current information about any restrictions. If you cannot move your plants, you may be able to take a cutting. Put the cutting in sterile soil or in a plastic bag with a damp cloth. It will survive for several days.

On moving day, pack your plants in any box of the proper size. Pack paper around the pots to keep them in place. Cushion branches and leaves with soft paper. Punch air holes in the sides of the box and fasten the lid loosely.

More detailed information on preparing your plants for moving can be found in Chapter 9.

Records, tapes and CDs—Use small cartons. Pack tapes and CDs in their holders. Pack records on end in a bundle.

Silverware—Use cloth or low sulfur content paper to wrap your silverware to prevent tarnishing. Wrap the chest in a blanket or moving pad. Put in the bottom of a carton of similar items.

Stereo/Phonograph—Secure the arm and changer. Wrap the dust cover in a large towel, small blanket, or soft tissue. Place the unit in a carton. Mark "fragile" on the carton.

Tools—Wrap tools separately and pack in small cartons.

Water beds—Because there are several types of water-bed mattresses, it is best if you follow the instructions for the type you have (from your purchase literature or your local water-bed store). In general, however, you first need to drain your water-bed. Unplug the water-bed heater. Drain using a siphon, faucet adapter, or drain pump. A drain pump can be rented from a general rental outlet or a water-bed store. It will reduce the draining time by at least half. Once the mattress is drained, grasp the baffle system along with the external vinyl and fold the mattress about 20 inches at a time. Place the mattress in a large plastic bag and pack it in a large carton. You can use a blanket to provide more padding and protection.

Disconnect the heater from the control and carefully roll the pad. Wrap it and place it in a carton where it will not be crushed.

Moving DOs

- DO invest in the proper packing materials to protect your belongings.
- DO begin packing early.
- DO label every box. Mark two sides, in the same position on each box, with destination room and contents. Mark "fragile" on boxes that hold your breakables.
- DO use towels and linens as packing material to cushion breakables.
- DO pack heavy items in small cartons and lightweight items in large cartons.
- DO pack each box tightly so that contents will not shift.
- DO seal each carton securely with packing tape.
- DO pack one box of essentials for the new home that will be the first thing unloaded.

Moving DON'Ts

- DON'T pack china, lamp shades, etc., with newsprint. Newsprint smudges.
- DON'T pack flammables.
- DON'T neglect to protect mirrors, framed pictures, or other breakables. Mirror cartons offer the best protection.
- DON'T pack and move things you will not use after the move.

What NOT to Pack

Whether you are driving the truck yourself or having a mover transport your goods, some items should not be moved because of the danger of fire or explosion.

These flammable items include aerosols such as hair spray, shaving cream, or deodorant cans; cleaning products, insecticides; and others. Other flammables include car batteries, bleach, gasoline, kerosene, propane or oxygen in tanks, oil-based paints, paint thinners and turpentine, lighter fluid, matches, and ammunition. Carefully review your belongings for these and any other combustibles.

Refillable propane tanks must be purged and sealed by a propane gas dealer. Discard any nonrefillable tanks.

For your safety, the safety of your belongings, and the safety of the truck driver, eliminate these items before moving day and plan to replace them as needed at your new home. It's inexpensive insurance!

Your Survival Box

Actually, you may decide your family needs more than one survival box. Tailor this idea to your needs. Basically, your survival box should include the things you and your family members consider essential upon arrival at your new home. Some suggestions are: coffeemaker and coffee, flashlight, important telephone numbers, a small household tool kit, matches, paper towels, a few linens, toilet paper, hand soap. You get the idea. This box is just for the things you may need immediately upon arrival.

You may allow each family member to pack a small survival box that includes a few personal items also, such as toothbrush, toothpaste, and other overnight-bag things. If your family includes a baby or very young child, consider taking a few familiar, loved items that the youngster can see and use the first few minutes in the new home. What you want is to make the first few hours in the new house more pleasant and less stressful.

Load your survival box either at the back of the truck for first removal (clearly marked, of course) or take it with you in the cab of your rental truck or in the trunk of your personal car. If you take a few minutes well before moving day and list out what should go into your survival box, you can ease the transition into your new surroundings.

What a Pack-and-Stack Service Will Do

It's pretty clear from the name of the service. If you plan to load and transport your goods yourself, but you hate packing or your time is limited, check around. A local pack-and-stack service will be happy to help out.

A pack-and-stack service will come into your home and safely pack all your belongings into the proper boxes and cartons so that your things will arrive at your new home unscratched and unbroken. When you call, ask about their experience, what materials they will use, and how they charge. Typically, a pack-and-stack service will charge by the box or carton packed, as do most moving companies.

How Your Mover Can Help

Your mover will be happy to assist you in any way with your packing. If you want to do all the packing yourself, your mover will assist you in determining your packing material needs and will offer the materials to you at a fair price. If, after reading this chapter and surveying your home and possessions, you want to let the mover do it all, your mover will bring an experienced packing crew to your home and have the job finished in just a few hours. They can complete the job quickly because they have the experience and knowledge (many packers specialize in one area of your home), they have probably worked together on many jobs, and they are objective (they won't get sidetracked looking through the picture album).

Even if you want to do the majority of the packing yourself, you may want to call on your mover to pack fragile and valuable items such as mirrors, paintings, collections, electronics, and art objects. And if you plan to pack it all yourself, but run out of time, give your mover a call. You can probably get last-minute help to make sure you meet your deadline.

Commonly Asked Questions

Q. Give me some packing guidelines.

A. Here are our 5 Rules for Perfect Packing:

1. Plan It All on Paper.
2. Use the Best Packing Materials.
3. Start Packing Early.
4. Mark Each Box with Its Destination and Contents.
5. Establish a Staging Area.

Q. What are the best packing materials and where can I get them?

A. The best packing materials are those that are made specifically for the purpose of packing and moving or storing household possessions. Your mover or truck rental company probably offers strong cartons, dish packs, wardrobes, mirror boxes, and other specialty packing items. If you value your possessions, it is worth the expense to purchase such materials. You may also be able to buy them secondhand, but in good condition. You will also need packing tape (not just masking tape) for sealing boxes, rope for tying off your load, and marking pens. If you question the prices your mover charges, check elsewhere. Even if you are using a moving company, you do not have to purchase your supplies from them unless they are doing the packing for you.

Q. What is a staging area?

A. Your staging area is the place you designate for storage of boxes and cartons that are completely packed, sealed, marked, and ready to load onto the moving truck. Keeping them all together will simplify loading them onto the truck and will also keep the mess in your home at a minimum.

Q. How many boxes will I need?

A. You can make an educated estimate of how many boxes, cartons, wardrobes, and other packing materials you need. Survey your home and then study the chart in this chapter. Or ask your mover or truck rental company to assist you in determining your needs.

Q. What items should not be packed?

A. Anything flammable should not be packed. The back of the moving truck can get hot and fires and explosions do occur. Safely discard any flammables before you pack and replace them as needed after you arrive at your new home.

CHAPTER 9

Making the Emotional Move

Moving is a huge physical job, but it is even more. It is an emotional chore. Changing residence appears as a stress factor on any test or chart measuring personal stress. In addition, several other factors that often accompany a move cause enough stress to appear on stress-assessment tests.

Some of those other factors are a change in job, change in school, change in church and organization affiliation, divorce, death of a family member, obtaining a mortgage, change in recreation activities, change in social activities, change in work hours or conditions, change in number of family get-togethers, vacation, marriage, retirement, and change in financial state. These and other changes that often occur as a result of moving from one home to another add to the stress of an already busy life.

For your family's emotional health, take the time during the moving process to reduce the stress on each family member. In this chapter, you will find a number of hints that will help eliminate the chaos and smooth the way for the emotional move from one home to another or even from one country to another.

Saying Goodbye

Rituals help us get through many of the hard times in our lives. Funerals are not for the person who died. They are designed to help the mourners say goodbye and begin the process of healing. Moving is a time of saying goodbye. Neglecting to say goodbye to the old home, friends, and town can leave an emotional gap. Saying goodbye can help bridge the gap and speed along the process of settling happily into your new home.

Think now about the goodbyes that you and the other members of your family will face.

Saying Goodbye to Relatives and Friends

The hardest goodbye is the one to the important people in your life who will not be nearby after your move. Plan to say your main goodbyes before the last few days prior to moving when you will be swamped with work and buried in the confusion of packing.

Have lunch with old friends and coworkers during the few weeks before your move. Plan an informal gathering with your neighbors a month before you leave. Organize a family reunion. Talk with your pastor well before you move for help through this emotional upheaval. Let people in your church group, civic organizations, sports teams, and other groups know you are leaving. Some may want to plan a going-away party for you—let them. You'll enjoy it and take good memories with you.

Each member of the family needs the chance to say goodbye to relatives and friends. Help your children plan their goodbyes. Young children may want to take cupcakes, cookies, or fruit and vegetable snacks to school, day care, or a play group a few days before leaving (don't make it the last day; that's too hard on you). Preteens or teens may want to have a Friday or Saturday evening party to gather friends for a send-off. Let them do most of the planning. They can even ask their guests to help supply snacks and beverages and to clean up afterward to eliminate extra work for the family who already has enough to do getting ready for the move. Again, don't make the party too close to moving day, unless a friend wants to host it at his or her house. Accept any help that is offered!

Many kids will have one, two, or three special friends they need to say a more private goodbye to. Let them or help them prepare a special lunch or treat them to lunch at a local restaurant. Depending on your budget, you might even spring for a few hours at a local amusement park or other attraction as a special treat.

Plan to keep in touch with close friends. We all have good intentions and tell lots of people we will write or call and we mean it at the time. Realistically, however, few of us are good at personal correspondence and it may be too costly to call often. But it is worth every effort to stay in touch with close, or "for-life" friends. Give them your new address and telephone number as soon as you have that information. Otherwise, before you even leave home, you can address postcards to those few special people and as soon as you have a new address and telephone number, jot it down and send it off. Think how nice it will be to receive a newsy letter from your old friends!

☞ **Money-$aving Tip #34** *Keep in touch economically with old friends through letters instead of expensive phone calls.*

Saying Goodbye to Your Old Home

If you have been happy in your old home and have loved living in it, saying farewell to it will be difficult, too. For many families, the house holds memories of hundreds of special occasions and even not-so-special occasions. If your home has been your safe haven, it may be scary to leave, not knowing if your new home will offer the same kind of security.

Each member of your family will have special, private places in the home that are more important. Your teenager may consider her bedroom her own private world that will soon be lost to her. You must allow her the time and privacy to part with that dear old friend in her own way. You can, however, also reassure her that she can create the same kind of special cocoon in your new home. If you already have the new house picked out, try to get photos of each room so that each family member feels a little familiar with the new place. With that photo and the dimensions of the room, your teen can plan where her furniture, posters, and other possessions will go. She can think about colors when the time comes to paint, and decide on curtains for the windows.

Maybe Uncle Bob lives with you and spends hours every evening and weekend in the basement creating furniture and toys with his woodworking tools. He will need extra time to lovingly pack up and say goodbye to his warm, familiar work space. It will be easier if he knows that the new house has a workshop in the garage just waiting for him to move in and make it his.

Saying goodbye is a combination of saying goodbye to the old and planning the new.

Take Memories Along

If you don't already have lots of pictures of friends, family, the old house and neighborhood, as well as favorite spots around town, get out the camera now and use a few rolls of film. Take candid shots of all the people you will miss. Get the "real people," not stiffly posed models. You can either get the film developed and into an album before you move, or you can take it along and get it developed as a treat soon after you move into the new house. Encourage your kids to get school pictures of all their friends and give them a holder for those photos. Make sure all photos are marked. We think we'll remember things forever, but in a few years when you go through some of those photos, you may be hard-pressed to name the people or the places, let alone remember when they were taken.

Go to the visitor center in your old hometown and pick up brochures and other information to take along as reminders and also to show new friends and neighbors where you moved from.

Take cuttings of special plants from the yard and the house if you are not moving houseplants. If you can't take cuttings because of the season or because of where you are moving, take pictures.

As you go through the process of moving, think about the things that have been especially meaningful to you in your home, neighborhood, and town. Take pictures, take samples, and store the memories in your head. If you enjoy writing, keep a journal.

Focus on the Benefits of Moving

If you look, you and every member of your household, even the one least happy about moving, can find a number of benefits to moving.

Moving can offer a new start, an adventure, an avenue to new friends, hobbies, and interests, and a learning experience. It's all in the attitude. While recognizing that moving is stressful and may lead to negative emotions, keeping the focus on the positive aspects of the move can help everyone involved get from here to there with the least stress and un-happiness.

Make Your Move a New Start

Someone in the family may need a new start in an area of his or her life. Making a move, especially if it is to a new neighborhood or town, can offer a fresh start. If a teen in the family has run into problems at school or otherwise, offer help in seeing that moving to a new school and town can give the chance to change behaviors and reputation. New surroundings and a clean slate may be all that is needed.

A child who has few friends because of shyness will have a whole new chance to practice assertiveness skills with new friends. Make sure this child knows as much about the new school and neighborhood as possible before moving. Role-playing going to school for the first time and meeting new people is often quite helpful.

If the move is because Mom or Dad has taken a job, it may lead to a new career and more satisfaction with life.

Look at your move as a beginning rather than an ending.

Make Your Move an Adventure

Even if you are simply moving to a new house within the same town or even the same neighborhood, you can make the moving experience an adventure. There will be a new home, yard, or maybe even acreage to explore, get to know, and make your own. Each family member can participate. Encourage everyone to spend some time in the empty house before anything is unloaded from the truck.

Slowly wander through the house. How can you use this room? The fireplace will offer warmth and comfort on cold nights. The basement may offer a playroom, party room, or family room that can be used in different ways through the years as the kids grow from toddlers to adolescents to young adults. A room or corner of the basement might be turned into a darkroom for the amateur photographer who has always wanted to try developing film and printing pictures. With a little work, the attic may provide a quiet space for sewing or for the teen who wants a unique room away from the rest of the family. Let your imagination loose.

After everyone has had a chance to explore the house and grounds, get together and share your impressions and ideas. You will be surprised at all the ideas that emerge! Most will probably never materialize, but even if just one or two become family goals, you will be well on the way to making the new house your own home.

Make the Trip to Your New House a Vacation

If your new home is more than a few miles from your old house, make the trip at least a minivacation. If the home is halfway or all the way across the country, make the move a real or even extended vacation.

Even if your drive will be just four hours long, find something along the way to stop and see, preferably something that will be new and fun for the whole family. Plan a picnic at a state park and rent a canoe for an hour after lunch. Stop at a hands-on science museum. Take the scenic route (if you're not driving a large rental truck or pulling a big trailer). Check out the local tourist information office and find one or two things to make the drive fun.

If your drive is longer, it will be easier to find things to do along the way. Pay attention to your budget if that is a concern. A few hours at even a small amusement park can get costly. Send for tourist information for any state you will be passing through. Look at commercial amusements and at natural attractions. It will be well worth an extra day to drive through Yellowstone or along the Grand Canyon. Find some natural caves to explore or stop for a swim at Salt Lake. Drive some country roads if you will be in the northeast in the fall and see the spectacular fall colors. Take along snacks, drinks, games, and other activities depending on the ages of the travelers.

You might even let your teenagers plan, or at least tentatively plan, your itinerary. Give them some guidelines such as budget for entertainment, time on the road, how far out of the way you will travel to see the sights, and what attractions along the way you want to see. You may need to plan the basic route, with each night's destination, and let them find a fun distraction for each day. Once the itinerary is complete, check it over to be sure it meets all your needs, including something you know each family member will enjoy.

Have a good vacation!

Think about Your Move from Your Children's Perspective

Moving upsets everyone. Routines change. Emotions boil. Fears emerge. Confusion reigns—especially in children. Most children dislike moving, yet about eight million of them move with their families each year.

A family meeting provides a positive atmosphere for telling your children about an upcoming move. Calling a family meeting or raising the topic of moving in a regularly scheduled family meeting will give the announcement about moving the importance it needs and the children will appreciate being included in the business of the move.

Tell your children the reason for the move. Tailor your explanation to the age. The youngest children only need to know that Mommy or Daddy has to work at a new office in a new town or that the family needs to be closer to Grandma and Grandpa to help them. Older teens will want and deserve to know more. They can understand that the family needs the increased income of a better job or that Mom or Dad will have better job opportunities in a larger city. They may not like it, but they will understand it.

Let the children ask any questions they wish and answer them as fully as you can, given their level of understanding. Be prepared for negative reactions. Children seldom like change. Try to maintain a positive attitude yourself, but don't sugarcoat the subject. Moving will probably be difficult for your children. Let them know you understand that and will help them in any way you can to make the transition. Tell them the advantages of moving.

Hold a series of family meetings during the moving process. Keep everyone up-to-date on plans and tasks. Keep everyone involved. Let the children help make some decisions. If possible, take them house-hunting with you or at least take them to visit the new house once you have found it. Ask them what they would like in a new house. If they cannot visit, try to get photos of the new house so everyone can begin to get to know it.

If the move is to another city, get information about your new hometown to share with the kids. If it isn't too far away, make a visit. Tour the neighborhood and the city. Find some city parks. Visit a museum. Tour the children's new school. Point out where Mom or Dad will be working. Find an attraction that you can promise to visit as soon as you are settled in the new house.

After the move, your children may need help adjusting to the new home, routine, school, friends, and other parts of their lives that have changed. You can help by settling into a family routine in the new home as quickly as possible. Make the routine as close as possible to the routine at the old house. Have meals at about the same time, keep bedtimes, and other familiar activities. Expect that the adjustment will take longer than you think it should. Unless serious problems occur, allow your children up to a year to become fully adjusted. If after a reasonable amount of time your children are still unsettled, ask their doctor to recommend a specialist to help solve any residual problems brought on by the relocation. If your move is the result of divorce or death, your children will benefit from counseling even before the move.

No matter what their ages, your children will need your help coping with the stress of moving.

Helping Your Young Child Cope

Very young children (under age five) do not necessarily need to know about your upcoming move as soon as you make a decision. In fact, telling them too far in advance will do no good and may even make the move seem unreal to them if you talk about it for several weeks before it happens. Put off telling very young children until the last two or three weeks or until the unusual activity in the house, such as serious packing, begins.

Home provides everything that is important to most preschool children. As long as the family remains intact, most preschoolers will focus on the loss of their familiar *home* rather than friends or other outside influences. Young children may not want to move into someone else's house and have strangers move into their bedroom and the rest of their home. Play-acting the move with dolls, a few boxes, and a wagon or toy truck can help children visualize moving.

Very young children need lots of reassurance. Tell them repeatedly that they will be moving with you. Three-year-old Amy knew her family had to give away their dog when they moved to a new home. She feared that because she too was a small member of the family, she may also be given away. Only with lots of reassurance from Mom, Dad, and her big brother was she convinced that being left with Aunt Sandra for moving day was not a trick to leave her behind permanently.

If a young child likes playing with his day-care center friends, try to settle him into a new day-care situation quickly. Young children make friends quickly.

Young school-age children usually have stronger friend-ship bonds and also take longer to make new friends. You can help them by checking the neighborhood for children near their ages, learning if their new school has an orienta-tion program for new students, and getting them involved in after-school activities. Elementary students are probably the only family members who will find it easier to move during the school year.

Helping Your Older Child Cope

Teenagers find moving more difficult. Their focus will probably first be on the friends and secondarily on the activ-ities they will have to leave behind. For them, summer offers the easiest transition because they probably have fewer ac-tivities and obligations. It should be easier for teenagers to meet friends in the summer and ease into the larger scene at school with those new friends' help in the fall. That way, your teens will be in on the beginning of the school year when friendship groups form, sports start, and clubs re-group. It is also easier to start junior high or high school at the beginning of a term rather than join a class halfway through its curriculum.

Your teenagers may surprise you with their outrageous behavior after being informed of a family move. At a time when teenagers need to begin taking control of their life, be-ing forced to move feels like a loss of control. Against their will, your teenagers will have to lose old friends and make new ones. They may have to quit their jobs and search for new ones in the new neighborhood or town. They may have to say goodbye to their first love. You can help by giving them support, space to explore and adjust to their feelings, and involvement in the move.

Young children focus on the loss of their room and home, adults focus on the physical move, and teenagers focus on the emotions that moving brings. Typically, teens will be shocked and angry upon learning of your upcoming move. These feelings may even lead to depression and panic and may last from the time of learning about the move to moving day and even beyond. These feelings are helping your teenagers to disconnect from the old life and prepare for the new. You can help by knowing what to expect, explaining to your teens that the emotions they feel are normal, and allowing them to talk about their feelings.

After the physical move to the new house, your teenagers will soon start to get used to the new home, school, neighborhood, and town, but it will take 6 to 18 months before they really feel at home. Teens may have roller-coaster emotions after the move, loving the new place one day and hating it the next. Eventually, the good days will far outnumber the bad days.

Teens seem particularly vulnerable, partly because they often do not take the best care of their bodies. Encourage your teens to eat well, get plenty of rest, and exercise—they'll be better equipped to cope with the inevitable stresses of moving.

Talk to school counselors and teachers. Schools work at different paces. Find out where your teen is in comparison to classmates and arrange for help in any needed areas. Make sure the school knows of any medical conditions that may need attention during school.

Help your teenagers get involved in your new neighborhood or town. Go to church as a family and find out about teen groups. Suggest they volunteer to help coach a young baseball team or help out at a nursing home. Encourage them to try the sports that are most popular in your new area as well as getting into old favorites. Discover together what makes your new hometown or state unique.

Letters from old friends help. Supply paper, envelopes, and stamps and remind your teenagers that they will probably not receive many letters if they do not write many. If your budget allows, let your teens make a few phone calls to old friends. Depending on budget and distance, consider bringing old friends to visit or sending your teens back to visit after a few months. It will provide something to plan and look forward to. And your teens may just come home again realizing that the new place is now more home than the old one.

When a Teen Wants to Stay Behind

When you announce your plans to move, your teen may at first flatly refuse to go along. Most, however, reluctantly come around after a while. Occasionally, though, an older teenager may stick to the idea of staying behind when the family moves to a new location. What can you do if your teen is serious about staying?

First, discover why your child wants to stay behind. Some reasons are valid; some are not. Your teen may simply want to stay with familiar friends or remain on an athletic team. Or he may want to assert his independence and punish you for moving. He may want to gain more freedom or finish a special program at the old school and graduate with his class.

If your teen is a senior or other reasons for wanting to remain in the old hometown or neighborhood are valid, you may agree to explore the possibility. With your teenager, list all the options available: He can move now; finish the term and then join the family; finish the school year at the old school; or complete high school before joining the family. Where would he live? With a relative or friend? In an apartment?

What will it cost? Is your teen willing to take on a part-time job to help pay any extra bills?

If you and your teen decide that staying behind is the best all-around solution, you will need to set some ground rules that are clearly understood and agreed upon beforehand by everyone involved: you, your teen, and anyone who will be responsible for your teen. You will want to make it very clear who pays for what. What household chores will your teen be expected to perform? When is curfew? Will your teen go to church? How will routine medical needs as well as emergencies be handled? Write out a contract that everyone signs.

☞ **Money-$aving Tip #35** *If your teenager has a good reason to remain in your old hometown, you may be able to work a deal with a friend or relative to provide the teen a home at little additional expense to the family. Your teen can probably find a part-time job to help toward any such expenses.*

Preparing Those with Special Needs

Moving can be especially trying to those with physical, mental, or emotional limitations. Because their needs are so individual, you will want to consult with their medical professionals to determine the best way to explain the move and to learn what special preparations need to be made. In some cases, counseling even before the move may be indicated. You will also want to request referrals to specialists in your new town and to find out what services are available there. As with moving anyone, the least disruption to their daily routine is desired.

Moving Your Pets

For many people, there's no question; when they move, their pets move. If your move is only a short distance, it's relatively simple. If your move is across country, it will be more difficult to take the dogs and cats, but it can still be done comfortably.

Local and State Regulations on Moving Animals

Most U.S. communities have ordinances regulating pet control and licenses. Check with the city clerk in the city to which you are moving to learn the local animal ordinances. You also need to contact the Department of Agriculture or the State Veterinarian's Office of the state where you are moving to learn your new state's animal entry laws. A few states have border inspection stations, but most rely on your compliance with the law. Depending upon your destination, you will want to carry the following items with you when traveling or moving with a pet.

Health certificate—Most states require a health certificate for entering dogs and horses. Many (about half) require certificates for cats, birds, and other household pets. If you have any question about your pet's health, take your pet to your vet early so that any problems can be cleared up in time to issue a health certificate for the time of the move. Some states require that the health certificate be less than ten days old. Remember to ask your veterinarian for a copy of your pet's medical and inoculation records and for a referral to a veterinarian in your new city.

Permit—You will need an entry permit to allow your pet to enter some states. Either you or your veterinarian can apply for this permit, which may require a fee. A health certificate may be needed to apply for the entry permit.

Rabies tag—Nearly all states require dogs and cats to wear valid rabies tags on their collars. These dated tags are issued when your pet is inoculated against rabies.

Identification—When traveling, a cat or dog should have identification attached to its collar. Birds should have identification on leg bands. Include your animal's name, your name, and your *new* address on this tag.

Using a Pet Transportation Service

A pet transportation service will make all the arrangements and handle all the details of moving your pet from one home to another. Your mover can probably recommend a reputable service. You may want to visit the facility and talk with several members of the staff before turning over responsibility for your beloved pet to them. Ask detailed questions. How will your animal be restrained? How long will its trip take? What food and water will be available? Who will handle your pet? How much experience do they have? Will your pet be around other animals? Do they require health certificates on every animal they handle? How much are their fees?

Once all your questions are answered and you feel reassured that your pet will receive VIP service, you can attend to other details of your move.

Sending Your Pet by Air

If your pet must travel by air to your new home, have it checked by your veterinarian and get any needed inoculations, a health certificate, and any medications your pet needs. Make flight arrangements early and ask about special requirements. You will need an FAA-approved animal crate. Whether your animal travels onboard with you or as air freight, clearly mark the words "LIVE ANIMAL" on the outside of the carrier.

If your pet is small (generally requiring an FAA-approved carrier no larger than $21'' \times 18'' \times 8''$), you may be able to take it into the passenger cabin with you as long as the maximum number of animals inside the cabin has not been reached, your pet is odorless, and not offensive to others. Arrive early, as most airlines operate on a first-come, first-served basis for allowing animals in the passenger cabin. If you must change airlines during your trip, be sure to check regulations with the second airline, as there generally is no through-checking of animals between airlines.

The only exception to animals being crated in the passenger cabin of an airplane is for Seeing Eye Dogs. Although regulations vary among airlines, usually a Seeing Eye Dog will be allowed to sit in the aisle of the cabin at the owner's feet. The airline must be notified *in advance* that the dog will be on the flight.

If your animal is too large to go into the passenger cabin or if you are traveling by another means and want to send your pet by air, most dogs and cats can be sent air freight. The Animal Welfare Act prohibits any air transport of kittens and puppies under eight weeks old. Check with the airline for regulations and for details concerning other pets, such as birds and rodents.Tropical fish should only be shipped after packing by a professional who specializes in tropical fish. Most airlines will not ship snakes.

Make arrangements for shipping your pet as early as possible. You will be required to prepay the shipment fees. On the day of the flight, feed the animal lightly at least five hours before the flight and water at least two hours before the flight. Walk your pet on a leash at the airport, if possible, and give any medicine. Be sure to have the animal's health certificate, permits, rabies tag, and identification tag available.

Place your pet in the approved shipping container, clearly marked "LIVE ANIMAL," and include your name, address, and telephone number, as well as those of the person who will meet the pet at the end of the flight. Attach the animal's leash to the outside of the carrier. Of course, unless the flight is very short and you can be at both ends, you will need to make arrangements for a good friend to either send the animal off or pick it up at the destination. Be sure that you or your friend picks up your pet on time at the destination. Any animals not picked up after about 24 hours can, at the owner's expense, either be shipped back to the point of origin or placed in a kennel.

If possible, ship animals only during moderate weather. In fact, some airlines will refuse to ship animals if it is cooler than about 45°F or over 85°F.

Even horses can be shipped as air cargo, but it is expensive and requires that someone travel with the animal. The horse will need a shipping stall approved by the airline and maybe even a loading ramp. Shipping charges must be paid in advance and tack must be handled separately.

Taking Your Pet in the Car

Most likely, your beloved pet will travel with you in your personal vehicle. Your animal will be more comfortable and happy with you, and it is far less expensive than sending it by air. Again, be sure your animal is in good health and carry any required health certificate, permit, identification, and rabies tag.

If your pet is not used to riding in a car, take it on several short trips and work on its travel manners. This will be easy if your dog has been obedience trained. To safely travel in a car, your dog should be trained to sit or lie down quietly. An alternative is to keep the dog in a crate. If your trip will include overnight stops, you should take a crate anyway so that the dog has a familiar space and a place where it can be confined in motel rooms.

Cats usually hate to ride in a car, but they will settle in eventually. They are safest, and usually happiest, crated. They like having a cozy, close place to nap.

If your pet gets carsick easily, ask your veterinarian about medication to help the condition. It also helps to feed very lightly or withhold food until the day's drive is completed.

Make sure your pet has its collar and tags in place and never let it loose while traveling. Even a well-behaved dog may bolt when let loose in a strange place. Cats can be taught to walk on a leash and will not be lost if they are only taken out on one. As when traveling with small children, plan plenty of rest stops to let your pet exercise and relieve itself. Be a responsible animal owner and only let your pet out in appropriate places and clean up after it. Keep your pet under control at all times and don't let it annoy others.

Remember your pet when you make motel, hotel, or campground reservations. Many places accept pets, but some do not, and those that do may have certain restrictions. Ask ahead of time.

Never leave any pet in a completely closed car. Even in cool weather, on a sunny day the temperature inside your car can reach killing degrees. If you must leave your pet alone in the car, park in the shade and open each window an inch or so. Never leave an animal alone in a car in hot weather.

Make a list of things you need to take for your pet. Include any prescribed medication, water, food, and a can opener if needed, dishes, leash, paper towels in case of motion sickness, and a scoop and plastic bags for cleaning up after your pet. If your trip is more than just a couple hours, you may want to also include one or two toys, treats, brush, and flea spray. If you will be staying in a motel, take your animal's regular bed or a carrier.

Most small pets (guinea pigs, hamsters, etc.) and birds travel best in the cages they live in at home. Make sure they have plenty of water; those tiny bodies dehydrate quickly. Keep your bird's cage covered to help it remain calm. Take care to keep birds out of drafts and extreme temperatures. Feed as usual.

With care, tropical fish can be moved by car; the shorter the trip, the better. Unless your aquarium is five gallons or less in capacity, your fish will travel more safely in another carrier. Half fill with water from the aquarium a plastic bag or an *unbreakable* container such as a bucket with a lid. Remember, your delicate fish need a fairly constant water temperature, so a styrofoam cooler will make a good holder. Carefully transfer the fish (being careful not to overcrowd) and close the container. Fish need air, so open the container every few hours to renew the air supply.

The easiest way to move your horse may be to tow it in a trailer behind your own vehicle if you are accustomed to towing a trailer. Horse trailers can be rented. If your trip requires motel stops, check beforehand to be sure you can park a trailer with a horse in the parking lot overnight. The horse will be fine in the trailer overnight. If you are camping, be sure horses are permitted in the campground. Another alternative is to board the horse at stables along the way.

☞ **Money-$aving Tip #36** *The most economical way to move family pets is with you in the car or truck. Avoid fines and other added costs by making sure you know the animal regulations of your new city and state.*

When the Pets Can't Go

When you simply can't take one or more of your pets with you, start early to find them a new home. Don't just give your animals away to someone you don't know. Too many animals end up as research subjects or in animal shelters.

Advertise your pet in the local media. Post a notice on your veterinarian's bulletin board. Make it clear that you will only place your animal in a good home. Spend some time with any prospective new owners. If you don't feel confident they will treat your pet well, wait; someone else will come along who will love your pet as much as you do.

If you have trouble finding a home, find out if there is a local adoption agency for pets. Some communities have a society that will even find foster homes for animals while they search out loving adoptive homes. Ask your veterinarian, groomer, obedience teacher, and others to find out if there is such a group in your area.

Moving Your Houseplants

Here's the best advice about moving houseplants: Don't. Either give them away or sell them instead. Most moving companies will not transport plants more than 150 miles, and they will not guarantee their condition upon arrival. Plants can be difficult to move and take up a lot of space in your vehicle. And you must check with the U.S. Department of Agriculture for regulations about moving plants into your new home state. If you decide you must move some of your houseplants, the following guidelines will help ensure success.

Three weeks before moving—Repot into unbreakable plastic pots any plants you will be taking.

Two weeks before moving—Prune as appropriate. Your plants will take up less space and be healthier.

One week before moving—Eliminate insects and parasites. Either carefully use a commercial insecticide, or better, place each plant in a black plastic bag for five or six hours along with a flea collar or pest strip.

A couple of days before moving—Water all plants normally.

One day before moving—If your drive is short, wrap the base and loosely wrap the top of the plant with damp newspaper, then wrap the whole plant with plastic. If your trip is longer, use dry newspaper around the bottom and soft, dry paper to cushion the branches. Place the plant in a moving carton and use more packing material as necessary to cushion the plant and hold it upright in the box. Cut holes in the sides of the box to provide air and fasten the lid loosely. Label the carton. Hanging plants can also be hung on the metal rack in a wardrobe carton.

During the move—Try to pack your plants in the interior of the car, as they may get too hot or too cold in the trunk. Plants won't survive overnight in the trunk of a car in Wyoming in the winter. If you must load your plants into the back of a moving truck, load them last and unload them first. During the summer, park in the shade and open windows a crack; in the winter, park in the sun and keep windows closed. If you stop overnight, take the plants inside. Unless your trip is more than four days, you do not need to open the cartons. If your trip is longer, after about four days, open the cartons and check to see if your plants need water.

Upon arrival—Unpack plants as soon as you can. Open boxes from the bottom and lift the carton off the plant to avoid damage. Place your plants for the light they need and try not to move them soon. They need to rest and acclimate. Don't you wish you could do the same?

How *Your Agent Can Help*

Real estate agents are well aware of the stress involved in moving and the emotional impact it can have on family members. They have helped many other families reduce the worries of moving and your agent wants you to have a stress-free move. Let your agent know what parts of the move are causing you stress. Give your agent a chance to help. Each agent has developed a host of resources for people on the move and will be happy to help you if possible.

How Your Mover Can Help

Most moving companies and national truck rental companies offer lots of help. When you ask any mover for a bid, ask for brochures they have on making your move easier so that you have more than one perspective. Many have comprehensive, illustrated brochures packed with helpful hints on all aspects of moving. Some even include activity books and other aids to help explain the move to the kids, get them involved in the move, and occupy them during the drive. Several movers also offer information on the emotional aspects of moving, as well as guidelines for preparing and moving kids, the elderly, the disabled, pets, plants, and other special topics.

Commonly Asked Questions

Q. How can I minimize the stresses of moving?

A. Plan everything. Learn all you can about moving and about your new house, neighborhood, city, and state. Involve the whole family.

Q. Why make such a big deal out of saying goodbye?

A. It's very difficult to start into, enjoy, and reap the benefits of a new home and life if you have not said goodbye to the old. Letting go of the old (but not forgetting) clears the way to embrace the new.

Q. When should I tell my kids about the move?

A. That depends on their ages. If your children are younger than about ten, they don't need a long lead time to worry about the move. Tell them two or three weeks in advance or when it becomes obvious that changes are occurring. If your children are older than ten, tell them as soon as you know. They need time to digest and adjust to the news and time to tidy up their own lives in preparation for the move.

Q. My younger children seem to be adjusting well to the news of our move, but my teenager is troubled. How can I help?

A. Open up a dialogue. Listen. *Really listen.* Let your teen air his feelings. Make sure he understands the need for the move. Cut him a little slack. Give him extra time to adjust. Get all the information you can about the new school. Find out about the soccer team or the skateboard park or whatever might interest your teen. Help plan a going-away party. Recognize that your teen will focus on the emotional aspects of the move: leaving friends, school, teams, clubs, etc.

Q. My teen says she won't move. What can I do?

A. Why does your teen want to stay behind? Is she about to graduate? Is she involved in a special activity that will not be available in your new town? If her reasons are valid, explore all the options. Consider letting her finish the school term or the year.

Q. Even though I am going to a new, better job, I am sad about this move. Why?

A. There are positives and negatives to every move. You see the benefits: a better job, maybe more money, new opportunities. But you are also leaving friends, perhaps family too, and familiar surroundings. You are probably apprehensive about some aspects of the move, whether it be finding a new running companion, compatible church home, or friendly neighborhood. Try to focus on the positives, but allow yourself to feel the inevitable sadness about what you are leaving behind and will miss.

Q. I have pets to move. What do I need?

A. You may need any or all of the following: a certificate of health, rabies tag, ID tag, and entry permit for a new state. Your veterinarian can help with all of this.

Q. How can I get my pet from Maine to Missouri?

A. You can take your pet with you in your personal vehicle, you can ship many pets via air (either as freight or in the passenger cabin with you), or you can hire a pet transportation service to handle it all.

Q. Why not move all my household plants?

A. Many household plants are delicate and difficult to move. They may not survive the move. Anything but very small plants will take up a lot of space in your truck or car. Most movers have restrictions about moving plants, and many states prohibit the importation of plants from another state. Often it is easier to give away or sell your plants (or at least all but a treasured one or two) and start over in the new house. Besides, your household plants can make great good-bye gifts to special friends.

CHAPTER 10

Moving Out and Moving In

If you have thoroughly organized your move and followed your plan, the actual move out and move in will still be plenty of work, but should not be so overwhelming physically or emotionally. When it comes right down to moving time, you still have to load everything on the truck, do final goodbyes, and clean up the old house. At the other end, you will have to unload, say hello, and unpack, maybe after first cleaning, painting, and repairing or remodeling the new house.

Dealing with Last-Minute Crises

You can almost count on at least one crisis to occur on your last day at the old house. It will probably only be a minor crisis, but on moving day it will seem insurmountable. Not so! When the Alexander family moved from the

Midwest to the Northwest, their crisis happened after the house was clear and everything was loaded in the truck.

Dad asked 12-year-old Brendon to straighten up the cab of the truck for departure. He did a great job. He cleaned out one side of the rental truck, then locked the door and went around to the other side. He cleaned that side, locked the door, and returned to the house—without the only key. Yep, the key was on the dashboard. Of course, it was a Sunday.

Coat hangers don't work to get into those truck cabs, which is comforting to know as long as the keys aren't locked inside. After lots of advice and attempts at help from neighbors and several phone calls, a towing service arrived and, for a modest fee, popped the door open easily and quickly. Crisis over. The Alexanders were on their way.

Unless you are lucky, something unexpected will happen on your moving day. Your strongest helper won't show up, or your car will have a dead battery, or Susie will get sick, or. . .

You can handle it. Call your helper; maybe he just over-slept. Take your battery to a service station for a recharge. Call a relative or good friend to take care of Susie for the day. If you have organized your move carefully, chances are any crisis you encounter on moving day can be solved without disrupting the move.

Stay calm. Keep in control.

Moving Out

By the time you get up on the morning of moving day, all your boxes should be packed and nearly everything ready to carry out and load onto the truck. You've arranged for utilities to be shut off. You've cleaned and defrosted the refrigerator. You've arranged for a friend to keep the dog for the day and another friend to keep the baby.

Eat a good breakfast and make sure that everyone else does, too. Strip all your beds. Send the dog and young children off with a hug and a kiss and reassurance that you will pick them up by dinnertime or by bedtime. Older children can help, whether you are moving yourselves or having a moving company do the job.

Let's look at what to expect during this busy day.

What to Expect from the Moving Company on Moving Day

If you have a moving company doing the loading, your job for the day consists of supervising and answering questions for the movers. They will do all the heavy work, unless you have arranged with the moving company to do the packing and/or loading yourself to keep costs down.

Stay with the moving van driver as he makes an inventory of your possessions. You can make notes on the inventory about the condition of any items. Read the bill of lading carefully before you sign it; it is the contract between you and the moving company. Put the bill of lading with your other valuable papers. You need to keep it until your possessions are delivered and the bill paid. If there is any dispute, the bill of lading will be needed for settlement.

Be sure the driver has detailed directions to your new home as well as the address and a telephone number in case he needs to contact you. If you will be on the road, give him a message phone where someone will have your travel itinerary and be able to reach you. The moving company office should have this information also. Confirm with the driver the date and time of delivery of your goods to your new house.

If you are paying a moving company to do the job, conserve your energy and let them do the hard work. They have the tools and the know-how to make quick work of disassembling beds and loading appliances. Before the truck leaves, take a last walk through the house to make sure they loaded everything that should go with the moving van. You probably won't have room in your car or suitcase for any overlooked items.

Also, be careful not to let them pack the things that are going with you in the car. Set them aside, all together, clearly marked for personal transport. Moving company packers will move everything. They have even been known to carefully package up trash, because their job is to pack, not to sort or decide what goes and what stays. When the Baxter family moved from Topeka to Chicago, ten-year-old Michael came home from his last day at his old school while the packers were doing their job. As usual, he dropped his jacket just inside the front door. He never saw it again until all the boxes were unpacked at the new house in Chicago!

If You Are the Mover

Moving day will involve more work if you are moving yourself with a borrowed or rented truck or trailer. Make sure your helpers are early risers. An early start to the day will help things go more smoothly. Entice them with coffee and bagels.

Pick up the moving vehicle early (if not the night before). Know beforehand who will do what. If there is last-minute packing (and there will be!), assign one or two people to handle that task. Another duo can disassemble and prepare beds. Have a set of basic tools handy. The children can run errands, carry light boxes, help load the car, serve refreshments, and help in many other ways.

One or two people with a dolly can move out lots of boxes quickly. Let the strong young men do the heaviest work, such as moving appliances and lifting heavy boxes. Have someone who has experience moving, or at least someone who has read the information in Chapter 6 on packing a truck or trailer, supervise the actual loading. Avoid the temptation of just loading whatever happens to come out of the house next. Careful loading will ensure safe arrival of your belongings.

Keep the crew working, but allow occasional breaks and keep snacks handy to keep energy flowing. Put on some upbeat music. Stop for a satisfying lunch. Healthy sandwiches, fruit, and vegetables will restore energy better than a fat-laden hamburger and french fries. Offer a continuous supply of nonalcoholic liquids.

Preparing Your Appliances for Moving

If you are taking all or some of your appliances with you, they will need some special care to make sure they arrive in good working condition. If your appliances are old or unreliable, consider leaving them behind and purchasing new or good used ones on the other end of the move.

If you do take appliances, take the time and trouble to prepare them. It is discouraging to load the washer for the first load in your new home and find that it does not work. Also, know what power sources are available in your new home. You might consider selling your gas clothes dryer if your new home only has electricity. Check with your moving company or an appliance company for the proper materials for securely anchoring your appliances, especially for a long-distance move. Your mover or appliance expert can also do this task.

Washing machines—Turn off faucets, disconnect hoses, and drain them. Place plastic bags securely over the ends of each hose to prevent leakage. Read your manual to learn how to brace the tub and secure the motor.

Refrigerators/Freezers—Follow the manufacturer's directions for defrosting your refrigerator or freezer. Dry the interior of the cabinet thoroughly (leaving the doors open for several hours will help), and load in an upright position (laying it on its side could damage it). To keep the interior smelling fresh, place a handful of fresh coffee, baking soda, or charcoal in a sock and place it in the cabinet. The cabinet can be packed with large, lightweight items.

Dryers—Check your manual or ask your appliance serviceman. You may need to secure the motor to prevent excessive movement.

Sewing machines—No special care is required for a short move. For a long-distance move, pack paper in and around the machine.

Stoves—Disconnect from electrical outlet or gas line. Shut gas line and cap tightly. Pack removable parts of electric ranges, including coils, separately.

Television sets—Some experts recommend service before and after moving. Read your owner's manual. Pack portable televisions in original cartons if available.

Cleaning the Old House

If you have been renting your old home, you may have a cleaning deposit to recover upon moving out. While some of the cleaning may have been done during the moving process, it's actually pretty easy to clean once everything is moved out.

Be sure your cleaning supplies do not get loaded on the truck! You will need your vacuum, mop, broom, rags, bleach, all-purpose cleaner, and any specialized cleaning products that help with your particular house. One or two good friends may volunteer to help. Let them! The work will go quickly then.

Many areas of the house, such as bedrooms and the living room, may not need more than vacuuming. Or, they may need walls washed, carpets cleaned and paint touched up. Allow time for these extra tasks. Wash down kitchens and bathrooms with bleach water or other disinfectant. Two people, working inside and out, can make short work of a houseful of windows.

Even if you do not have a cleaning deposit on your home, it is courteous to the new owners or renters to leave the house clean and tidy. The new occupants would also appreciate a folder containing the owners' manuals and any other information you have on appliances, etc., that stay with the house. You can include a list of local repairmen and information on utilities if you wish. Just think how helpful it will be if someone moving out of *your* new home leaves the same kind of information!

Once the truck is loaded and the house is all clean, take a final walk through each room, the attic, basement, garage, yard, and any other areas where any possessions could still be hiding. Check all closets and look behind doors.

☞ **Money-$aving Tip #37** *Take the time and effort to recover any cleaning deposit on a home or apartment you are renting. If you figure your hourly rate for cleaning, it's well worth it.*

Now, you're ready to lock up, head for the motel or a friend's house, and get a good night's rest before hitting the road to your new home. Or, you're ready to head to the new neighborhood and your new house if your move is local.

What to Take with You

Even if your move is short, you will want to be sure that a few items go in the car with you or will be the very first things unloaded off the truck so they are available immediately in the new house. Naturally, the longer the trip to your new home, the more items you will need with you.

First of all, you will want to take maps, snacks, and a first-aid kit. Take an emergency road kit that contains flares, a flashlight, and tools. You will want to carry your valuable jewelry, stocks, and other such items with you. Be sure to take your credit cards, checkbook, and cash or traveler's checks. You will also want any other necessary papers such as pet health certificates, prescriptions, and passports and visas if you are leaving the country. Take your camera and film or camcorder. If a moving company is transporting your belongings, make sure you carry all the paperwork pertaining to your shipment. Carry an ample supply of any medications you may need along the way.

If you are driving more than a couple of hours with children, take games, books, and other items such as personal stereos or cassette players. Take writing paper or notes, stamps, and envelopes so children can write to friends they are leaving. Give each child a small box or bag to fill with whatever they think they'll want for the trip. For an overnight or longer trip, pack all toiletries and clothing you will need, plus a little extra just to be safe.

What will you need for the first few hours at the new house? A coffeemaker and coffee, mugs, toaster, toilet paper, and a few cleaning supplies. Think about your family and your new house as you decide what to take in the car with you. Keep a list in your moving notebook, which, of course, will go with you in the car, too.

Add to or subtract from the following list to create your family's moving kit:

❏ Valuables such as coin collections, silver, jewelry
❏ Prescription medications and written prescriptions
❏ Sunglasses
❏ Camera and film
❏ Clothing for trip and first few days at new house

❏ Snacks/drinks/water
❏ Paper plates/cups/plastic silverware
❏ Paper towels
❏ Credit cards/cash/checkbook
❏ Toys/games/personal stereo/books
❏ Writing paper/envelopes/stamps
❏ Pet supplies
❏ Address book
❏ Extra car keys
❏ First-aid kit
❏ Tool kit
❏ Flashlight with batteries
❏ Maps
❏ Papers for new house
❏ New house keys
❏ Moving papers
❏ Linens for new house
❏ Alarm clock
❏ Cleaning supplies
❏ Hand soap/towels
❏ Trash bags
❏ Telephone and answering machine to hook up immediately at the new house

Take Frequent Breaks from the Car

Stop often, especially if your trip is lengthy. It may take an extra hour or two to reach your destination each day, but you will be more rested. Stop at a local market and pick up picnic items, then stop at a rest area or city park for lunch or dinner. Try carrying a cooler with fruits, cut-up vegetables, granola bars, juice, pretzels, and other easy, nutritious foods for breakfast and lunch, then stop for dinner at a restaurant.

Get out of the car when you stop to check out historic signs or views. Stretch, walk, do a few exercises, and change drivers if possible. Make sure the kids get out, too. Urge them to run and play for a few minutes. Take the dog or cat out for a walk.

Keep Your Possessions Safe

Be sure the cargo door of the truck is always locked with your own padlock. Also, lock the cab when you leave the truck for even a brief time. Close windows all the way unless you have pets inside. Whenever you stop at night, try to back up your truck to a wall so that the cargo door is not accessible. It is also a good idea to check the cargo periodically to ensure that nothing has shifted. A shifting cargo means unsafe driving as well as possibly damaged goods.

Keep a Record of Your Trip

Use a section of your moving notebook for a travel journal. Each evening, record what you did during the day: what you saw, how far you traveled, where you ate. Keep a record of all your expenses (remember, some are tax deductible) and save the receipts. Also write down your feelings about what you did during the day, what you feel about leaving the old home, and what you feel about approaching the new home. One family member can serve as scribe for the entire trip, you can take turns each day, or everyone can write a brief account each day. Depending on your children's ages, they might like to have diaries of their own. In a few years it will be fun to reread your journal and remember the trip and your feelings about moving.

Saying Hello to Your New Home

At last—you're home. At your *new* home.

Of course, it doesn't have any furniture yet. Maybe even no draperies. But if you've been organized, the electricity and water are on. It's time to say hello.

Whether you are renting or buying the house, whether you have seen it before or not, wander through the house. Get each family member to do the same. This may be the first time you have seen it without furniture. Imagine it with your belongings. See the living room with your oak and glass. Or imagine the master bedroom with your antique brass bed. Take your time. Examine all the nooks and corners, all the cupboards and closets.

On this first exploration, look at the positives and the possibilities. Soon enough, you will take another look to see what needs to be cleaned, repaired, painted, or remodeled.

☞ **Money-$aving Tip #38** *If your new home needs a thorough cleaning and you want to pay to have it done, schedule the cleaning* before *you move anything in. A professional cleaning crew can zip through very quickly without any furniture or boxes in the way.*

Spend time in each room. How do the windows open? You might want to air out the house right now. Where is the thermostat that controls the furnace? Where does the laundry chute come out? What's behind that door? Is there room over the mantle for your favorite painting? Think again about furniture placement.

Look through the attic. Can you safely store your treasures here? Could you someday add a bedroom or a personal retreat? Visit the garage. Is there a workbench? What might you store in those cupboards? Is there room to hang the bicycles on the wall and still get both cars in? Where can the lawn mower go?

Once you have become acquainted with the interior of the house and garage, tour the yard. Where will the swing set go? Is there room for croquet or frisbee? Is there a garden space already established or a sunny spot where you can test your green thumb? Is the yard fenced for pets and small children? If so, is the fence in good repair? Children and animals will find any weakness.

Take the time to walk around the neighborhood. You might be able to spot or meet potential friends. Toys in the yard indicate children who might be around your own youngsters' ages. A boat or classic car in the driveway lets you know someone nearby shares your interests. Introduce yourself to anyone you meet. You might just stumble upon a park where you can picnic and where your kids can play. Or you might discover an old-fashioned neighborhood grocery store where you can pick up last-minute items for dinner.

If you still have some time and energy left, get in the car and drive around town. Show the kids their school. Find the nearest supermarket and pharmacy. Beginning to get to know your way around will help you feel comfortable quickly in your new home and town.

Your pets also need to get to know the new house, yard, and neighborhood, but it may be easier to wait until after the truck is unloaded and the extra people gone. A frightened cat or dog could bolt out an open door and get lost.

Before you take your pet in the house, give it a chance to relieve itself. Then, be sure all doors are closed. Windows, too, if it is a cat. Take the animal in and let it explore its new home. Decide where the animal will eat and set out fresh water. If it is near mealtime, go ahead and feed it. If it's not near mealtime, offer a treat. If the yard is safely fenced, let your dog explore there, too. If the yard is not fenced, take the dog out on a leash. Even cats that normally spend lots of time outside should be kept inside until you feel sure they understand that the new house is home and will stay close and return at least at mealtime. Most dogs will also enjoy a walk through the new neighborhood, on a leash of course.

Before Unloading the Truck

Whether you have driven a truck and everything is sitting out in the driveway already, or the moving company van is arriving tomorrow, you will probably want to at least do some cleaning before anything is moved in. If the house needs more than just cleaning, you may have made arrangements to store your belongings temporarily and stay in a motel while you do or have someone else do the work.

Get everyone involved in the cleaning chores. Even small children can sweep decks and sidewalks and perform other simple tasks. They will be busy and feel more ownership of the home if they are allowed to help.

If the house is empty, cleaning should go quickly. An alternative is to hire a local cleaning firm to come in and wash walls and other surfaces, scour bathrooms and kitchen, vacuum and shampoo carpets, and scrub other floor surfaces. Get an estimate—it might not be as costly as you think, and it certainly will simplify your move. The service can even do the job before you arrive, so that when you walk in you see everything shiny and clean and smelling fresh.

When the Moving Company Arrives with Your Possessions

Be at the house ahead of the movers. If you are moving into an apartment building, be sure to make prior arrangements for using the elevator to bring your things in. Put signs on every door or doorway with the same designations that are on the boxes: "Master bedroom," "Study," "Baby's room," and so on. The task of unpacking will be greatly simplified if all boxes are placed in the correct rooms as soon as they come off the truck.

If you moved across even one state line, you must pay for your shipment when it arrives. Have all of your paperwork available.

If you have young children to occupy while the movers bring in all your goods, you might hook up the television and VCR first thing and play a favorite old movie or one that you rented. By the time the movie is finished, there may be boxes in their new bedrooms that they can unpack.

Know approximately where you want things placed. To avoid confusion, have one person supervise the unloading and answer questions for the movers. Let the movers be the ones to position the sofa under the picture window. They will also reassemble anything, such as bed frames, that they disassembled for loading. If you have planned your furniture placement in advance, you will have little heavy moving to do after the crew leaves.

As the truck is unloaded, inspect large items and any boxes or cartons with obvious damage. Note any possible new damage on the inventory. Check off everything on your inventory to be sure that absolutely everything arrived. Otherwise, it could be months later, when you are preparing a dinner party for your new friends, before you notice that your best serving dishes did not arrive or broke during the move. Open cartons that contain anything of great value before the driver leaves. Sign your inventory after everything has been unloaded and inspected. You will need it if you have to file a claim for lost or damaged goods.

Unloading Your Rental Truck

Again, organization is the key. As previously mentioned, label each room with the same designations you used when marking all your boxes. Appoint one person to supervise. Avoid the temptation to just get everything into the house and worry about placement later. In the long run, you will save time and energy if you place your furniture where it will stay and carry boxes into the rooms where they will eventually be unpacked.

☞ **Money-$aving Tip #39** *Be sure to unload your rental truck promptly and return it on time to avoid any extra charges.*

Save your back by using the proper tools. You can unload faster and with much less effort with a utility dolly and an appliance dolly.

Set up your beds early and grab that last-loaded box that contains bedding and other essentials. Make up your beds. You will be glad later! After a hard day of unloading and unpacking, it's no fun to sleep on the floor.

☞ **Money-$aving Tip #40** *Make setting up and making your beds a priority upon moving into the new house. Doing so can save a night's motel bill.*

After the Truck Is Unloaded

Once the truck is unloaded, whether you unloaded or supervised, take a break. Make some coffee or get a soft drink. Congratulate yourselves on your safe arrival. The mountain of boxes may look insurmountable, but it's not.

Make sure there is toilet paper, soap, and paper or real towels in each bathroom. Put paper cups, soap, and towels in the kitchen. Check to see that each room has adequate lighting. Who wants to stumble around an unfamiliar room in the dark, especially one with stacks of boxes on the floor!

Hang a shower curtain if needed. A hot shower before bed or upon rising will feel wonderful.

☞ **Money-$aving Tip #41** *Make a trip to the library near your new home. Some have framed art that you can borrow just like a library book. It can help to make your home more complete until you can choose and purchase your own art.*

Don't try to do it all in one day. It will probably take several weeks before all the boxes are unpacked and you feel really settled and "at home" in the new house. If you unpack just a few boxes each day, the mountain will quickly become a molehill.

Feeling at Home

It's time to begin making the new house feel like your home and the town, if it is new, like it is your hometown. The sooner you get a few familiar objects out of boxes and around the house, the sooner you get to know the neighbors, and the sooner you officially become a member of the community and/or the state, the sooner you will begin to feel like you belong. Here are a few things you can do to get started:

- ❏ Hang your favorite picture.
- ❏ Hook up your stereo.
- ❏ Buy a couple houseplants or plant a tree or bush in the yard. As the years go by, you can measure its growth from the time you moved in.
- ❏ Put your name on the mailbox.
- ❏ Pick up any mail held at the post office and start home delivery.
- ❏ Register to vote.
- ❏ Get a new driver's license if you changed states.
- ❏ Change the registration on your car if you changed states.
- ❏ Post telephone numbers of the hospital, police, and fire station.
- ❏ Find out about trash pickup and recycling.
- ❏ Knock on your neighbors' doors and introduce yourself and your family.
- ❏ Keep on exploring your new neighborhood and town.
- ❏ Host a neighborhood barbecue or brunch.

☞ **Money-$aving Tip #42** *Watch the mail in your new mailbox for coupons and discounts from nearby supermarkets and other businesses welcoming you to the area.*

Helping Your Children Feel at Home

Your children will probably need your help to feel comfortable in the new house. You've already made arrangements for their new schools. How can you help them adjust? Here are a few ideas to try.

❑ Unpack some favorite toys immediately.
❑ Maintain a daily schedule as close to what the children were used to at the old house.
❑ Learn about local activities for children: swimming, Little League, story hour at the library, day camps, Bible School, park and recreation department programs, afterschool activities, whatever your children might be interested in. They may need strong urging to take the first step into the unfamiliar.
❑ Make sure your kids meet local children. Find out which neighbors or coworkers have children close to your children's ages. Invite them to your home.
❑ Make time for your children to share their feelings with you, especially their sad or scared feelings. Share *your* feelings with them so they'll know you understand.
❑ Encourage your children to keep in touch with friends from your previous neighborhood or town. They can write, call, or even e-mail.

Some Final Moving Tips from Those Who Know

Professional movers and frequent movers have learned many ways to make moving easier, quicker, and less expensive. You can make your move easier by using just a few of their suggestions. Some are reminders from throughout the book and others are new ideas. Here are their secrets:

- ❏ Organize. Organize. Organize. The better planned your move, the less stress you will suffer.
- ❏ Get rid of furniture that's too large or won't coordinate with the new house.
- ❏ Seriously consider replacing rather than moving appliances.
- ❏ Don't forget to collect deposits from utility companies, etc.
- ❏ Ask for refunds from prepaid services.
- ❏ Use toll-free reservation numbers for making travel arrangements.
- ❏ Learn about long-distance telephone carrier options before you move. By doing so, you may save money on your first calls from your new home.
- ❏ Get any letters of recommendation that may be helpful in your new hometown.
- ❏ Write or call banks in your new town and request their newcomer kits.
- ❏ If you are moving because your spouse has been offered a new job, begin now to find your own niche. Ask if your spouse's employer offers aid to you in finding a position. If you don't already belong, join a professional organization. Use your network. Someone may know someone who. . .
- ❏ Call the local Welcome Wagon. They will bring you gifts, gift certificates, and money-saving discounts.
- ❏ Move midweek if you can. There will be less traffic, fewer people move then, and all the services you need

should be open. Also, move midmonth if possible because most people move at the end of the month.

❏ Don't plan to move the same day that the settlement on either the house you are moving out of or into closes. Delays do happen.

❏ Arrange to have phone service at the old house disconnected *after* you move out and connect service at the new house *before* you move in.

❏ Fully understand the estimate from your mover. Ask questions. Know exactly what is included in the price.

❏ Even if you are moving out of town, pack the white and yellow pages from your old area. You may want to call or write friends or businesses back there.

❏ If you have lots of books, research the cost of mailing them at book rate. It may be cheaper than shipping them with your household goods.

Enjoy your new home!

How *Your Mover Can Help*

If you hire a moving company, they will handle all the heavy work of moving your belongings out of the old house and into the new house. And you can leave the driving to them! As long as you contract with a mover you trust, you can relax during the move, knowing that your possessions are in good care.

You can also turn to your mover for many last-minute crises. A representative of your moving company can probably recommend specialists for crating your most delicate, valuable items and for safely preparing your appliances.

Even if you don't have a mover and you get into trouble at the last minute, you may be able to get help from the professionals. If moving day is approaching rapidly and you realize you will not complete all the work, call a few movers. If they are not booked solid, they can probably send a crew to your house to help with the final packing and loading. Or try a pack-and-stack service. You may pay a little higher hourly rate than if you had scheduled in advance, but it may make the difference in meeting your deadlines and getting to your new hometown in time for your first day at the new job.

Many movers now have customer service departments that offer services to reduce the stress of moving even more. Many have toll-free numbers you can call at any time of day or night to check on the progress of your shipment. You can also let them know if you, for some reason such as car trouble or another problem, will not reach your destination in time for your delivery date. Your mover will make arrangements, though probably at added cost, to hold your delivery temporarily.

Commonly Asked Questions

Q. What do I have to do on moving day if I have hired a mover?

A. You will need to be on hand to supervise and to answer questions. You will want to check the inventory of items going onto the truck and note their condition. Be sure the driver has your address, directions to the new house, and a phone number where you can be reached.

Q. *How can I make moving day easier if I am moving myself?*

A. Here's that word again: organization. An organized move is an easy move, at least comparatively. Have everything packed, marked, and ready to load before moving day. Have a small crew of good workers (either hired or volunteer). Assign specific tasks to each worker. Take breaks and keep up everyone's energy with snacks and meals.

Q. *How can I make the drive to the new house more pleasant?*

A. If your drive is more than a couple hours, take activities for the children and snacks and drinks for everyone. Take frequent breaks and get out of the car. Stop at local sights or attractions. Have a picnic. If your pets are with you, take food, water, and a leash. If your trip includes overnight stops, take clothing, toiletries, and more toys and activities.

Q. *What do I need to do on the day the movers deliver my household goods?*

A. Again, as on pickup day, you must be on hand to supervise and answer questions. You will probably have to pay in full for the shipment. You will want to check every item as it comes off the truck and note any damage or loss on the inventory, which you will then sign. You will tell the movers where to place your furniture. If rooms and boxes are labeled, the movers can take all boxes directly to the rooms where they will later be unpacked.

Q. *How can I make unloading easier if I am the mover?*

A. You can make the task easier by knowing where you want things placed in the house and directing your helpers. Bring the truck as close to the main door as possible and use the ramp. Offer snacks and beverages.

CHAPTER 11

Using Computers to Help You Move

The newest tool in the moving field is the computer.

That's right: the computer. The little machine that the kids have been using to play interactive video games and to surf the Net can be used by those over 21 to help them move.

Your computer can help you organize your move, find valuable resources, check out the latest products, get the best financing, and save you money on your move.

This chapter will show you how.

Getting on the Internet

The latest rage is the Internet. Advertisements for products on TV include their "Web site." Friends try to give you their "e-mail address." What does it all mean and, more important, who cares?

What does it mean? The terms used are simply words that help describe a new tool: the Internet. It's really no different than any other latest-and-greatest invention in that some people use it for good and others don't. The Internet is nothing to be fearful of. It is simply a tool.

Who cares? Contrary to what many folks say, you *can* live quite well, thank you, without access to the Internet. However, it is a tool that can help you get the information you need faster and, sometimes, more easily than in traditional ways. The printed word never replaced conversation as the primary tool of communication. Nor will the Internet replace the printed word.

Maybe the Internet is a tool that can help you make your move less stressful.

Understanding the Internet

So what is the Internet? It's an *inter*active *net*work of computers connected together through telephone lines. Think of it as a telephone system between computers. One computer calls another to find out what's new. It asks questions, answers questions, and spends a lot of time saying "uh-huh."

What You Need to Get on the Internet

You need a computer, a modem, some communications software called a browser, and a few bucks. The few bucks are so you can subscribe to an Internet provider or IP. An IP is a service that will connect your computer with other computers on the Internet. The typical charge is less than your monthly cable TV bill. Some charge by the hour and others have a flat monthly fee for nearly unlimited access, so check around for the best deal.

If you want to get onto the Internet, first find a local IP, then ask what software and hardware you'll need. They want you to become a subscriber, so they will typically help you get set up. Where can you find a local IP? Ask at local computer shops, check the classified ads in area newspapers, and ask friends.

Finding Things on the Internet

There are lots of areas on the Internet, many of them far beyond the scope of this book. The most popular—and the most friendly—is what's called "the Web." It's also known as the "World Wide Web" or WWW. In fact, many businesses include their Web address in advertisements and even on products.

For example, the Web site for the American Movers Conference is www.amconf.org/. What does that mean?

The first part (www) means it's a World Wide Web address. The next part (amconf) is the domain name, and the last part (org) means it is an organization site (gov would mean government).

There's a bit more to the address, however. To reach this location on the Internet, you need to tell the computer that you're using hypertext transfer protocol. What? Don't worry about it. Just prefix the address with:

>   http://

So, your uniform resource locator (URL) address to reach the American Movers Conference is:

>   http://www.amconf.org/

Type that Web site into your computer and watch the magic start.

Many moving companies already have Web addresses and more are being added every day. They tell about their services, offer pages of helpful information about moving, and some will even let you request a rough estimate of the cost of your move. Here are some other useful Internet Web addresses to help you make a stress-free move:

FIGURE 11.1 World Wide Web Addresses of Moving Companies

Web Address	Moving Company
http://www.americanredball.com/	American Red Ball Transit Co.
http://www.alliedvan.com/	Allied Van Lines, Inc.
http://www.alliedintl.com/	Allied International Moving Services
http://www.atlasvanlines.com/	Atlas Van Lines, Inc.
http://www.bekins.com/	Bekins Van Lines
http://www.globalvan.com/	Global Van and Storage South
http://www.invan.com/	Interstate Van Lines, Inc.
http://www.northamerican vanlines.com/	North American Van Lines
http://www.ryder.inter.net/	Ryder Consumer Trucks
http://www.stevensworldwide.com/	Stevens Worldwide Van Lines
http://www.uhaul.com/	U-Haul
http://www.mover.com/~tallmove/ companys/wheatonvanlines.html	Wheaton Van Lines

Searching the Net

Now that you're plugged in to the Internet, there is much you can look for. Searching or "surfing" the Internet is relatively easy and there are many tools available. Most Web browser programs offer you ways to search the Internet for key words.

The problem will soon become not how to find things on the Internet, but how to *selectively* find things. For example, asking for a search using the term "moving" finds literally thousands of Web addresses where the term is used. With practice and by reading the "help" screens, you'll soon learn how to find just what you're looking for. The Internet holds plenty of information on moving companies (you can locate Web sites for many large and small moving companies in addition to the ones listed previously). You can also search for other information on moving, including special topics such as moving the elderly, the disabled, and children.

☞ **Money-$aving Tip #43** *If you're hooked up to the Internet, you can save money on your move by researching all sorts of information about moving, such as housing prices in your destination city, moving companies, pet transportation services, and low airfares.*

Corresponding on the Net

Once on the Internet, you'll meet people and find a few new and old friends. How can you correspond with them? By using electronic mail or e-mail. Web browser programs usually have some type of e-mail writing and delivery system on them. Your IP can tell you more. In fact, your IP can give *you* an e-mail address.

For example, if your commercial Internet provider is named Harborside and your account name with them is Cottage, your e-mail address would be:

cottage@harborside.com

Folks who want to send you a message would do so using your e-mail address. And you would use their e-mail address to send them a message. It's like your street address or telephone number, except it's an electronic address.

Using Other Online Services

The Internet is a big network that nobody really owns or manages. You buy access time from those who supply the computer hardware and buy the telephone time to get on the Internet. There are, however, many commercial networks called online services.

The two most popular online services with consumers today are America Online (800-827-6364) and Compuserve (800-848-8199). Not only do they offer their own electronic resources, but both also offer access to the Internet through them.

These companies provide computer software that manages the connection and makes it simple for the user to move from topic to topic. Monthly subscription rates are usually about $20 and include some "free" time.

How Your Agent Can Help

Many real estate offices rely on computers and some are hooked up to the Internet. Ask if your agent has an e-mail address and/or a Web site.

Your agent should be able to help you house-hunt from Connecticut to Nevada via computer. Your agent will also probably have connections with other agents throughout the country to help you search for a new home quickly and easily. Some programs even include photos of available homes. With computers and fax machines, you no longer have to wait days for the postal service to bring photos and information. If you have a computer with online or Internet services at home or your office, your agent can send you information at any time.

If your agent is on the Internet, you can ask for a search on special topics on moving or just some general information. Your agent may also be able to recommend a good computer shop if you are interested in purchasing your own system.

Commonly Asked Questions

Q. *Can someone on the Internet access my computer?*

A. Not without knowing your passwords. If security is a concern, make sure your communications software and modem offer password protection. And make sure you don't give out your password to others.

Q. *How can I get information off the Internet?*

A. Most Web browser software includes features to let you download files or print information directly from the screen to your own printer. They use programs called file transfer protocol or FTP.

Q. *What are "newsgroups"?*

A. Newsgroups are groups of people who exchange information and chat among themselves on a common topic. There are newsgroups for homeowners, do-it-yourselfers, and thousands of other topics. To learn more about newsgroups, talk with your Internet provider.

Resources for People on the Move

Moving Companies

Allied Van Lines, Inc.
PO Box 4403
Chicago, IL 60680

American Red Ball Transit Company
PO Box 1127
Indianapolis, IN 46206-1127
800-877-7332
Fax: 317-351-0652

American Red Ball International, Inc.
PO Box 75986
Seattle, WA 98125-0986
800-669-6427
Fax: 206-526-2967

Atlas Van Lines, Inc.
1212 St. George Road
Evansville, IN 47711

Interstate Van Lines, Inc.
5801 Rolling Road
Springfield, VA 22152
800-745-6683

Paul Arpin Van Lines, Inc.
PO Box 1302
East Greenwich, RI 02818-0998
800-343-3500
Fax: 401-821-5860

Stevens Worldwide Van Lines
World Headquarters
527 Morley Drive
Saginaw, MI 48601
517-755-3000

United Van Lines, Inc.
One United Drive
Fenton, MO 63026
314-326-3100

Wheaton Van Lines, Inc.
8010 Castleton Road
Indianapolis, IN 46250
317-849-7900

National Truck Rental Companies

Ryder Consumer Truck Rental
2799 N.W. 82 Avenue
Miami, FL 33122
800-467-9337

U-Haul International, Inc.
2727 N. Central Avenue
Phoenix, AZ 85004
800-468-4285

Other Moving Resources

American Association of Retired Persons
1909 K Street, N.W.
Washington, DC 20049
202-872-4700

American Movers Conference
Consumer Brochure
1611 Duke Street
Alexandria, VA 22314-3482
703-683-7410
(Note: A consumer brochure on moving is available at no charge by sending a stamped, self-addressed, business-size envelope.)

American Society of Appraisers
PO Box 17265
Washington, DC 20041
800-272-8258
(Note: Request the "Directory of Certified Professional Personal Property Appraisers," a state-by-state listing.)

Gray Panthers
311 S. Juniper Street, Suite 601
Philadelphia, PA 19107
215-545-6555

Internal Revenue Service
800-829-3676
(Request Publication 521 titled "Moving Expenses.")

Interstate Commerce Commission
Headquarters Office
12th Street and Constitution Avenue, N.W.
Washington, DC 20423
202-275-7844

Interstate Commerce Commission
Regional Office
Room 16400
3535 Market Street
Philadelphia, PA 19104
215-596-4040

Interstate Commerce Commission
Regional Office
Suite 550
55 West Monroe Street
Chicago, IL 60603
312-353-6204

Interstate Commerce Commission
Regional Office
Suite 500
211 Main Street
San Francisco, CA 94105
415-744-6520

"Let's Get A Move On!" video
Produced by KIDVIDZ and Ryder
800-845-3636
(Note: This video of advice on how to make a family move an enjoyable experience is available from Ryder for a fee.)

***MOBILITY* Magazine**
800-372-5952
(Note: An index of MOBILITY *articles about relocation and children is available—document #18512.)*

National Council of Senior Citizens
925 15th Street, N.W.
Washington, DC 20005
202-347-8800

National Council on Aging
600 Maryland Avenue, S.W.
Washington, DC 20024
202-479-1200

Service Core of Retired Executives (SCORE)
1129 20th Street, N.W.
Washington, DC 20036
800-368-5855
Fax: 202-653-6279

U.S. State Department
Passport Office
900-225-5674

Pet Information Directory

Alabama
State Veterinarian
Dept. of Agriculture and
   Industries
205-242-2647

Alaska
State Veterinarian
907-745-3236

Arizona
State Veterinarian
602-407-2858

Arkansas
State Veterinarian
501-225-5138

California
State Veterinarian
Dept. of Food and Agriculture
916-654-0881

Colorado
State Veterinarian
303-239-4161

Connecticut
State Veterinarian
Dept. of Agriculture
203-566-4616

Delaware
State Veterinarian
Dept. of Agriculture
302-739-4811

Florida
State Veterinarian
Florida Dept. of Agriculture
   and Consumer Services
904-488-7747

Georgia
State Veterinarian
Dept. of Agriculture
404-656-3671

Hawaii
State Veterinarian
Dept. of Agriculture
808-483-7111

Idaho
Division of Animal Industries
208-334-3256

Illinois
Division of Animal Industries
217-782-4944

Indiana
State Veterinarian
317-232-1344

Iowa
State Veterinarian
Bureau of Animal Industry
515-281-5305

Kansas
Livestock Commissioner
Animal Health Department
913-296-2326

Kentucky
State Veterinarian
502-564-3956

Louisiana
State Veterinarian
504-925-3980

Maine
Director
Division of Veterinary Services
Dept. of Agriculture
207-289-3701

Maryland
State Veterinarian
Maryland Dept. of Agriculture
Animal Health Division
410-841-5810

Massachusetts
Bureau of Animal Health
617-727-3018

Michigan
State Veterinarian
Animal Industry Division
517-373-1077

Minnesota
Executive Secretary
Board of Animal Health
612-296-2942, Ext. 16

Mississippi
State Veterinarian
601-354-6089

Missouri
State Veterinarian
Dept. of Agriculture
314-751-3377

Montana
Dept. of Livestock
406-444-2043

Nebraska
State Veterinarian
402-471-2351

Nevada
State Veterinarian Director
Bureau of Animal Industry
Nevada Dept. of Agriculture
702-688-1180

New Hampshire
State Veterinarian
Dept. of Agriculture
603-271-2404

New Jersey
Division of Animal Health
Dept. of Agriculture
609-292-3965

New Mexico
State Veterinarian
Livestock Board
505-841-4000

New York
Division of Animal Industry
Dept. of Agriculture
518-457-3502

North Carolina
State Veterinarian
Dept. of Agriculture
919-733-7601

North Dakota
State Veterinarian
Board of Animal Health
701-224-2655

Ohio
Chief
Division of Animal Industry
614-866-6361

Oklahoma
State Veterinarian
Animal Industry Services
405-521-2840

Oregon
State Veterinarian
Dept. of Agriculture
503-378-4710

Pennsylvania
Director
Bureau of Animal Industry
Dept. of Agriculture
717-783-6677

Rhode Island
State Veterinarian
Division of Agriculture
401-277-2781

South Carolina
State Veterinarian
Clemson University
803-788-2260

South Dakota
State Veterinarian
605-773-3321

Tennessee
State Veterinarian
615-360-0120

Texas
Director
Animal Health Commission
512-719-0700

Utah
State Veterinarian
Dept. of Agriculture
801-538-7160

Vermont
State Veterinarian
Livestock Division
Dept. of Agriculture, Food and
    Market
802-828-2421

Virginia
State Veterinarian
Division of Animal Health
804-786-2481

Washington
State Veterinarian
Dept. of Agriculture, Food
    Safety
Animal Health Division
206-902-1878

West Virginia
State Veterinarian
Dept. of Agriculture
304-558-2214

Wisconsin
State Veterinarian
Dept. of Agriculture
608-266-3481

Wyoming
State Veterinarian
Livestock Board
307-777-7515

GLOSSARY

accessorial services Services other than actual transportation, such as packing, unpacking, picking up goods from a second location, etc. Charges for these services are *in addition to* transportation charges.

addendum (change order) A form used to amend the original estimate, usually due to changes in items to be shipped or services to be performed.

additional transportation charge (ATC) An adjusted charge that compensates the carrier when it performs services in areas where labor rates are higher than the national average. It also compensates a carrier for costs due to traffic congestion and for added time traveling for pickup or delivery.

advanced charges (third-party service) These are charges for services performed by others but arranged for by your mover. Charges will appear on your bill of lading. Typically these are for specialized services to prepare delicate or valuable items.

agent A local moving company with authorization to act on behalf of a national moving company.

appliance service The preparation of appliances that need special handling before shipping.

auxiliary service (shuttle) At times, a smaller truck (shuttle) must be used when a large van for some reason cannot travel the roads required to reach a pickup or drop-off point.

bill of lading The contract between you and the moving company. It also serves as your receipt for the possessions they transport for you.

binding estimate A written, guaranteed price for shipment based on an itemized list of items to be moved, the distance to be traveled, and services to be performed.

booking agent The agent who accepts your order for shipping and registers it with the van line.

bulky article Large items, such as cars, boats, and campers. An additional fee is charged for the difficulty of handling such items.

carrier The company actually providing transportation for your shipment.

claim Your statement of loss or damage to any part of your shipment.

C.O.D. (cash on delivery) Shipments that require payment upon delivery. Payment can usually be made in cash, traveler's check, money order, cashier's check, or credit card.

consignee The person who will accept shipment, whether it is the shipper or someone the shipper designates.

consignor The person from whom the shipment was picked up, whether it is the shipper or someone the shipper designates.

CP (carrier packed) Articles packed into boxes and crates by the moving company.

cwt. The shipping charge per 100 pounds.

deadhead Traveling empty. The miles a van must travel without cargo to pick up a paying load.

declared valuation Your claim of the value of the goods being shipped. This establishes maximum liability of the mover.

destination agent An agent at the destination who will assist you or the van operator.

elevator carry An extra charge that is added if a shipment must be either picked up or delivered with the use of an elevator.

estimate A moving company representative's estimate of the cost of moving your goods, based on weight and van requirements, as determined by a visual inspection of the shipment. See binding and nonbinding estimates.

expedited service Delivery on a specific date, as requested by the customer. An additional charge may apply.

extra stop Pickup or delivery at more than one point. Incurs an additional fee, regulated by tariff.

flight charge (stair carry) An extra fee for carrying large, bulky items up or down stairs.

gross weight The weight of the truck and contents after your goods have been loaded.

hauling agent The agent who owns the truck that will move your belongings.

high-value inventory Items that are worth more than $100 per pound, such as coin collections, furs, jewelry, or antiques.

ICC: Interstate Commerce Commission The federal agency in charge of the regulation of interstate transportation.

inventory An itemized listing of the items in your shipment, including notes on condition.

line-haul The tariff charge for transporting your goods from pickup point to destination.

long carry (distance carry) A charge added when goods must be carried an unusual distance from the truck to the house.

long haul Generally, a move that is more than 450 miles.

moving counselor The moving company representative who estimates the cost of your shipment and who will answer your questions about the estimate, services, or moving.

net weight The weight of your goods, found by subtracting the tare weight from the gross weight.

nonbinding estimate A price given to you before the move that does not guarantee the final bill. The final bill will be calculated on the weight of the shipment, the distance traveled, and the services performed.

operating authority Certification for a carrier to transport household goods between designated geographical areas.

order for service The paper authorizing the mover to move your belongings.

order for service number (registration number) The number assigned to your shipment. It is used for recordkeeping and tracking your shipment.

origin agent An agent in your area who will help with preparing your shipment (such as packing household goods) or who can provide information about your move.

overflow Items that are shipped on a second truck when space is unavailable on the first truck.

packed by owner (PBO) Items that you pack yourself.

peak season rates Higher rates that are sometimes charged during the summer.

pickup and delivery charges Transportation charges for moving your shipment between a temporary storage warehouse and your residence.

reweigh A second weighing of your shipment at your request or the mover's request.

road van A tractor-trailer that makes long-haul trips.

shipper You. The person whose belongings are being moved.

short haul A shipment of less than 450 miles.

storage in transit Temporary storage of your shipment at the moving company's warehouse.

straight truck A single cab and body vehicle.

survey The examination of your goods by the carrier's agent for making an estimate of shipping costs.

tare weight The weight of the truck and contents prior to loading your shipment.

tariff The carrier's provisions, including rates, for services performed during a move.

third-party services Services that are performed by someone other than the carrier, at your request.

unpacking Taking your things out of boxes and cartons and disposing of the cartons and packing materials.

valuation Your declaration of the value of the items being shipped.

van A truck that is used for moving.

van line The national moving company that oversees affiliates who transport interstate shipments.

van operator The driver of the truck.

warehouse handling An extra charge for placing and/or removing items from temporary storage.

INDEX

ABOUT THE AUTHORS

The CENTURY 21® System, recognized as the number-one consumer brand in real estate, has helped millions of people with their homebuying and homeselling needs for more than 25 years. In the relocation process as well, the CENTURY 21® System has assisted families every step of the way.

To meet the high expectations of today's demanding, value-conscious consumer, the CENTURY 21® System has redefined the real estate industry with innovative technology tools, strategic alliances with other industry leaders that offer a wide array of home-oriented products and services, distinct brands for special properties, and other housing-related opportunities.

Visit the CENTURY 21® System at *Century 21 Communities*^{SM}, the most comprehensive source of real estate and community information on cities across North America, on America Online® at **Keyword: CENTURY 21.** Or contact one of the System's network of 6,400 independently owned and operated offices throughout the United States and Canada, as well as in 21 countries around the world.

Judy Ramsey is an author, editor, and writing instructor with extensive experience in successful moves. In addition to *Century 21 Guide to a Stress-Free Move*, Judy has written on a variety of other topics for consumers and do-it-yourselfers.

CENTURY 21® is a registered trademark of Century 21 Real Estate Corporation. Each CENTURY 21® registered office is independently owned and operated.

Special Offer!

You get all this with an
ADT Security System

- Up to 20% savings on homeowner's insurance
- An exclusive 6-month, money-back service guarantee
- A system that can meet your needs and budget
- 24-hour burglary and fire monitoring

Installation Savings That Can Really Add Up

Save **$50** on an installation cost of $249

Save **$75** on an installation cost of $499

Save **$100** on an installation cost of $999 or more

To take advantage of this special offer call 1-800-221-6151!